EAT FRESH

QUICK AND EASY MEALS

CHEF TOM WOODBURY

FRONT TABLE BOOKS
AN IMPRINT OF CEDAR FORT, INC.
SPRINGVILLE, UTAH

ISBN 13: 978-1-4621-1446-7

Published by Front Table Books, an imprint of Cedar Fort, Inc.
2373 W. 700 S., Springville, UT 84663
Distributed by Cedar Fort, Inc., www.cedarfort.com

Library of Congress Cataloging-in-Publication Data

Woodbury, Tom, author.
Eat fresh : quick and easy meals / Chef Tom Woodbury.
pages cm
Includes index.
ISBN 978-1-4621-1446-7
1. Quick and easy cooking. I. Title.
TX833.5.W655 2014
641.5'5--dc23

2014010285

Cover and page design by Bekah Claussen
Cover design © 2014 by Lyle Mortimer
Edited by Deborah Spencer

Printed in the United States of America

10 9 8 7 6 5 4 3 2 1

TO LISA

CONTENTS

DESSERTS

INTRODUCTION

Food is personal and intimate. Although the phrase "you are what you eat" is frequently used to signify eating something less than healthy, in my opinion it illustrates how each and every meal we consume fuels and powers our body. In addition, the emotional response of smelling and tasting food fuels our soul. The magical ability of food to transform our mood is what drives a cook. It's what pushes us to make dishes that will not only sustain life, but that will also magnify the emotional well-being of those we serve the dishes to. With each bite, our attention and love is incorporated into the bodies and spirits of those we choose to share our food with. We cook because we love.

I've always felt that understanding food is the best way to adequately prepare it. Once I understand something, I can't help but love it. To that end, I've compiled some tips and tricks that will help you better understand food, and also learn to have that love for it.

Let's consider eggs for a moment. The egg is one of the most nutritional complete items on the planet. Why? Because the sole purpose of the egg is to provide nourishment to the embryo. It's designed to be food. The protein in an egg is so complete that the only whole food that absorbs into the body better is breast milk. Yet it's a food that we scarcely understand. Many myths and misconceptions exist about eggs. I've compiled several questions regarding eggs to help you in your attempt to prepare the perfect egg.

What method do you use to make a perfect hard-boiled egg?

A "perfect" hard-boiled egg is defined as an egg with a tender yet firm egg white, a creamy yet cooked egg yolk, and no green/gray ring around the outside of the yolk. The tricks to a "perfect" egg are the following:

» Buy your eggs one week before you plan on cooking them, this makes them easier to peel.

» Start your eggs in cold water, then apply heat. This minimizes cracked egg shells.

» Bring your water to a boil, then reduce the heat to just below a simmer. The hot boiling water sets the outside of the egg shell, making it easier to peel. Reducing the heat to just above a simmer keeps your yolk creamy.

» Immediately immerse your eggs in cold water. The cold shock reduces the green/gray layer around the yolk.

How do I make the best meringue?

Egg white proteins in their unwhipped state resemble a microscopic Slinky, waiting for the chance to be stretched. As the whisk agitates an egg white, the Slinky starts to stretch and bond with other egg white proteins, capturing air bubbles in the process and creating a tower of delicious egg white, perfect for a pie!

With just a few proper techniques, you can guarantee a perfect meringue every time!

One of the biggest challenges in making meringue is sugar. As the meringue cooks, the dissolved sugar loses moisture and crystallizes. These long strands of sugar crystals resemble the framework of a house, providing structure to keep the meringue from sagging once it is removed from the oven. The problem is that sugar also weighs down uncooked meringue, limiting its altitude. So how do you get maximum altitude, and still maintain the crucial structure? Simply add the sugar when the egg white reaches the soft peak stage. But the sugar presents another challenge.

Adding granulated sugar too late in the whipping process is risky. What if the sugar doesn't appropriately dissolve, and your velvety meringue is marred by pockets of large sugar crystals? When making a meringue, use powdered sugar. It dissolves instantly, and also includes small amounts of cornstarch to help with stability. When substituting powdered sugar for granulated sugar, 1 cup of granulated sugar equals 1¾ cups of powdered sugar (powdered sugar has a smaller crystal size, and therefore holds much more air).

But why does every meringue recipe I make call for cream of tartar? Cream of tartar is the salt of tartaric acid, a by-product of wine making. It has a pH of 5, and helps the tightly packed egg white open up and make the transformation into a long strand. This gives your egg whites volume because it allows them to capture more air. It also prevents the sugar in your recipe from forming large crystals, meaning a smoother meringue—the perfect meringue to put on a pie!

Speaking of pie, what about those little brown drops on my meringue? How do I prevent "weeping meringue?"

Even if your pie is made using the steps above, weeping can still be a problem. Weeping is caused by excess moisture in your pie escaping into the meringue after the meringue has started cooking. The cause of this moisture? Putting uncooked meringue on a cold pie. When meringue is put on a hot pie, the steam goes into the meringue and escapes before the eggs have a chance to set, thereby limiting weeping. But when meringue is put on a cold pie, the pie filling doesn't start to produce steam until the meringue has set. This means all that moisture is captured in the meringue and escapes in the form of little meringue teardrops.

What's the nutritional difference between a brown and a white egg?

Assuming the chickens laying the eggs are fed a similar diet, the difference between a white egg and a brown egg is the color of the egg shell. The majority of the nutritional content of an egg is caused by the type and style of feed given to the chicken.

If brown and white eggs are the same, why are brown eggs more expensive?

The chicken that lays a brown egg tends to be larger than the chicken that lays a white egg. Larger animals require more feed and are therefore more expensive to own. Simply put, brown eggs cost more to produce.

What about egg grades? Are two *A*'s are better than one?

To understand this, it's important to understand egg anatomy. There are 3 parts to an egg that impact its grade: the yolk, the amount of thick egg white it contains, and the amount of thin egg white it has. Yes, there is more than one type of egg white in 1 egg.

Grade AA eggs have the highest proportion of thick egg white and have a firm yolk with a strong membrane between the two.

Grade A eggs have a higher amount of thin egg white and have a well-formed yolk with a weak yolk membrane.

What does this grading mean when I'm cooking with eggs?

Grade AA eggs are perfect for any time when the yolk will not be combined with the egg white, such as poaching and over easy. Keep in mind that as an egg ages, the thick egg white is transformed into thin egg white. Therefore, fresh AA eggs are the best for poaching.

For all other uses, such as hard boiling, baking, scrambling, and making batters, you can use regular grade A eggs without impacting your recipe. A special note on hard boiling: eggs with a higher proportion of thin egg white are actually best for hard-boiling, since they minimize the amount of peel that sticks when you remove the shell. Also, with hard-boiled eggs, older eggs will always be better for peeling easily.

But there are *so* many more ingredients than just eggs in the kitchen. And with each and every item there is a misconception about what that ingredient is and what it can do. Most of this misinformation is put out there to help us feel better about what we are eating. But in reality, the label is rarely more than just marketing fluff. Take "all natural" and "cage free." These frequently misused terms offer little, if any, actual health benefits. To clarify these frequently applied insignias, I offer some clarifying information, as regulated by the USDA.

ORGANIC

In layman's terms, "organic" is a certification given by the USDA to foods that are produced without the use of banned substances, and in a manner that maintains an ecological balance. In order to understand what this means, we first need to consider the designations that the USDA uses to categorize organic food. Each category has its own set of rules regarding what makes it organic. Here are some of the key points of each category from their designations:[1]

Crops

A plant that is grown to be harvested as food, livestock feed, fiber, or is used to add nutrients to the field. To be certified as organic, it must be produced without the use of synthetic or sludge based fertilizers. The use of chemical pesticides is prohibited. Instead, baited insect traps or predatory insects and animals are frequently used to control unwanted insects. Lastly, the seed stock being used must be free of genetically modified seed.

Livestock

Animals, milk, or eggs that can be used for food or in the production of food, fiber, or feed. To be organic, they must be raised in an environment free of antibiotic and hormone use, fed a diet consisting of organic grass or feed, and given access to a pasture. The administration of approved medications generally have a "withdrawal period" prior to the animal being taken to slaughter, or milk being used.

Processed Products

Items that have been handled and packaged (like chopped carrots) or combined, processed, and packaged (like soup). To be considered 100 percent organic, the ingredients used in the process must be from an organic certified source. However, in certain instances ingredients not certified as organic may be used, if they are on the USDA approved list (items like baking powder and carbon dioxide).

Wild Crop

Plants from a growing site that is not cultivated. The harvest of the crop must be from an area certified to be pesticide-free for at least 3 years, be harvested with minimal impact, and promote future growth of the area to be considered organic.

Worthy of note, the USDA doesn't currently have a standard for organic fish, but when the standards of other countries are applied, "organic" fish are only fed organic food and are raised in a manner that maintains ecological sustainability.

There are other labels that can be applied to food that aren't necessarily regulated by the USDA.

Cage-Free

This label indicates that the bird is able to freely roam a building, room, or enclosed area with unlimited access to food and fresh water during their production cycle. This label is a voluntary label and is not regulated.

Free Range

This label indicates that the bird is provided shelter in a building, room, or area with unlimited access to food, fresh water, and continuous access to the outdoors during their production cycle. The outdoor area may or may not be fenced and/or covered with netting-like material. This label is regulated by the USDA.

All Natural

As required by USDA, meat, poultry, and egg products labeled as "natural" must be minimally processed and must contain no artificial ingredients. There are no standards or regulations for the labeling of natural food products if they do not contain meat or eggs.

Pasture-Raised

The USDA has not developed a labeling policy for pasture-raised products.

Humane

These labeling programs are not regulated by the USDA.

By understanding how these labels are applied, we can be better consumers. We can feed our loved ones in confidence, knowing that the food we provide will sustain both body and soul, both mind and spirit.

It is my hope that you're able to use the recipes in this book to continue to develop your love for food and to pass that love along to those you cook for. I've been told it takes minutes to learn to cook, but a lifetime to learn about food. Good luck on this journey. It will take you to fascinating places and flavors, and will ultimately make you a better cook.

1. "Electronic Code of Federal Regulations Part 205—National Organic Program," last updated April 9, 2014, accessed April 9, 2014, http://www.ecfr.gov/cgi-bin/text-idx?c=ecfr&sid=3f34f4c22f9aa8e6d9864cc2683cea02&tpl=/ecfrbrowse/Title07/7cfr205_main_02.tpl.

Breakfast

THE BEST WHOLE WHEAT WAFFLES EVER

MAKES 3–4 8-INCH BELGIAN WAFFLES

Normally whole wheat waffles are soggy and dense, but the inclusion of cornstarch gives this waffle a great crunch, and the apple cider vinegar makes them light and airy—you won't believe they're whole wheat!

¾ cup WHOLE WHEAT FLOUR
¼ cup CORNSTARCH
½ tsp. BAKING POWDER
1 tsp. BAKING SODA
1 tsp. SUGAR
¼ tsp. SALT
1–1¼ cups MILK
1 EGG
¼ cup OIL
1 tsp. VANILLA
1 Tbsp. APPLE CIDER VINEGAR

1. Preheat waffle iron.
2. Combine all dry ingredients and mix well.
3. Add milk, egg, oil, and vanilla, and mix well to combine. Add enough liquid so that batter makes a small mound or ribbon temporarily before returning to level.
4. If you're adding in additional fruit (blueberries, bananas, apples, and so on), do it now and gently stir.
5. Right before pouring batter onto waffle iron, add vinegar and mix quickly. Make waffles as per the instructions for your specific waffle maker.
6. Place on a cooling rack immediately after removing from waffle iron.
7. If you plan to freeze and reheat, wrap individually, and reheat in your toaster on a medium setting.

NOTE

» For blueberry waffles, add ½ cup fresh or frozen (and thawed) blueberries. For the strongest blueberry use smaller berries.

» For banana waffles, add 1 mashed banana and mix it in immediately prior to adding vinegar.

LEMON RICOTTA PANCAKES MAKES 8–10 4-INCH WIDE PANCAKES

If desired, this batter can also be dropped into a deep fryer by the teaspoonful to make delicious fritters.

¾ cup FLOUR
¼ cup CORNSTARCH
1 tsp. BAKING POWDER
½ cup SUGAR
4 EGGS
zest from 2 LEMONS
16 oz. RICOTTA, drained
dash of SALT
1 tsp. VANILLA

1. Combine flour, cornstarch, baking powder, and sugar and stir to combine. Set aside.
2. In a large mixing bowl combine eggs, lemon zest, ricotta, salt, and vanilla. Whisk or mix until completely smooth and lump free.
3. Add dry mixture to wet mixture and stir until it is lump-free again. Cover and store in fridge for at least 30 minutes.
4. Preheat a griddle or frying pan over medium heat.
5. Pour batter into pan using a ¼ cup.
6. When pancake starts to bubble on top and edges start to look dry, flip. Cook for 2–3 more minutes and serve.
7. Serve with Berry Coulis.

BERRY COULIS MAKES ENOUGH FOR 8–10 PANCAKES

Drizzle this on top of your lemon ricotta pancakes for a delicious contrast to the lemon.

1 lb. STRAWBERRIES, washed and stems removed
2 Tbsp. LEMON JUICE
¼ cup SUGAR
½ tsp. VANILLA

1. Combine all ingredients in a blender or food processor and process until liquid and chunk-free.
2. Strain through cheesecloth if desired.

GREEK OMELET MAKES 1 OMELET

The trick to a good omelet is cooking over low heat. The result is a tender egg that almost melts in your mouth.

1 Tbsp. OLIVE OIL
chopped ONIONS
handful of SPINACH
2 ARTICHOKE HEART PIECES, diced
2-3 LARGE EGGS, whipped
2 Tbsp. LIQUID (water, cream, or milk)
sprinkle of FETA
SALT AND PEPPER

1. Place a nonstick frying pan over heat, and adjust until a water drop vaporizes in 1–2 seconds. Add olive oil to pan. Add onions, spinach, and artichoke pieces, and cook until spinach is completely cooked.
2. Remove veggies from pan.
3. Combine eggs with liquid and stir.
4. Pour egg mixture into hot pan, and immediately start scraping sides to middle of pan and rotating pan until runny eggs take scraped eggs place. Continue this effort until eggs no longer fill in voids left as you scrape. Add cooked veggies on omelet, and sprinkle with feta cheese. Add salt and pepper to taste, fold, and serve.

BREAKFAST CHEESE SOUFFLÉ MAKES 4–6 SERVINGS

Here's my problem with traditional cheese soufflé recipes: it's all egg, and very little cheese. I decided it was time to make a cheese soufflé *filled* with so much cheese flavor that it can only be called "super cheese."

1 Tbsp. BUTTER, to grease ramekins
4 EGG WHITES
¼ tsp. CREAM OF TARTAR
¾ cup MILK
3 Tbsp. FLOUR
3 Tbsp. BUTTER
½ tsp. SALT
8 oz. TILLAMOOK SHREDDED SHARP CHEDDAR CHEESE
3 EGG YOLKS

1. Preheat oven to 375°F.
2. Generously butter 4–6 medium ramekins, at least 4 ounces in size.
3. Combine egg whites and cream of tartar, and whip until whites form stiff peaks.
4. In a 4-quart or larger saucepan, combine milk, flour, butter, and salt. Mix until flour is completely dissolved. Place pan over medium-high heat, mixing until butter has melted and sauce has thickened. Add cheese and mix until melted.
5. Remove from heat and spoon ¼–½ cup of sauce into egg yolks and mix well. Add mixture back to sauce and cook for 2 more minutes.
6. Separate egg whites into 4 equal portions. Add 1 portion of egg whites at a time to sauce, folding mix until egg whites are completely incorporated.
7. Add soufflé mix to each ramekin, filling it *just* below top of ramekin.
8. Place on middle rack of oven and bake for 20–25 minutes, until top is a deep brown and soufflé barely jiggles when moved.

OPTIONS

» Add ½ teaspoon dill with cheese.

» Add ½ teaspoon smoked paprika with cheese.

» After buttering, pour 1 tablespoon of parmesan cheese into each ramekin and tilt or rotate each ramekin until sides and bottom are coated in cheese. Dump out any excess.

» Serve with fresh green herbs such as chives, cilantro, or basil.

BAKED PROSCIUTTO EGGS MAKES 1 SERVING

Also called "shirred eggs," this method of cooking results in a tender egg topped with delicious melted cheese. It's unlike any egg you've ever tried.

- OLIVE OIL
- 1 slice PROSCIUTTO
- 1 slice HAM
- 1/4 tsp. minced ROSEMARY
- 1/2 tsp. minced SAGE
- 2 EGGS
- dash SALT
- dash PEPPER
- shredded MONTERREY JACK CHEESE

1. Preheat oven to 350°F.
2. Grease a 6–8 ounce ramekin with olive oil.
3. Add prosciutto and ham, and top with rosemary and sage.
4. Put a touch of olive oil on rosemary and sage.
5. Gently crack two eggs into ramekin.
6. Add salt and pepper.
7. Top with shredded cheese.
8. Place in oven for 18–20 minutes (cheese will be brown and a knife inserted into ramekin will come out clean).

FAUX SOURDOUGH WHOLE WHEAT PANCAKES MAKES 8–10 4-INCH PANCAKES

When adding the vinegar, it's fun to pull the kids around to watch as the dough nearly doubles in size. Be sure to make this recipe in a bowl with plenty of room to spare.

- 1 cup WHOLE WHEAT FLOUR
- 1/2 tsp. BAKING POWDER
- 1 tsp. BAKING SODA
- 1/4 tsp. SALT
- 1 Tbsp. SUGAR
- 1 EGG
- 2 Tbsp. VEGETABLE OIL
- 2–2 1/2 cups MILK
- 2 Tbsp. APPLE CIDER VINEGAR

1. Combine flour, baking powder, soda, salt, and sugar. Stir to combine.
2. Add egg, vegetable oil, and milk. Mix gently until combined. Batter should briefly form a small divot when your spatula is raised, and small drops of batter fall into mix. If small mounds/ribbons form, add more liquid.
3. Preheat griddle over medium heat (325°F).
4. Immediately before pouring batter onto griddle, add vinegar and quickly mix it in.
5. Pour batter on griddle in 4- or 5-inch diameter servings.
6. When pancake starts to bubble on top and edges start to look dry, flip. Cook for 2–3 more minutes and serve.

NOTE

» If including any fruit (bananas, blueberries, and so on), add to batter immediately prior to adding vinegar.

BAKED PANCETTA EGGS MAKES 1 SERVING

Pancetta is made out of the same cut of meat as bacon, but is compressed into a circle, making it the perfect shape to sit in the bottom of your ramekin.

2 slices PANCETTA
2 Tbsp. coarsely minced ARUGULA
2 EGGS
dash SALT
dash PEPPER
thinly sliced BRIE CHEESE

1. Preheat oven to 350°F.
2. Add pancetta to the bottom of a ramekin. (This version of baked eggs doesn't need oil as pancetta has enough to keep ramekin clean.)
3. Add minced arugula on pancetta.
4. Gently crack two eggs into ramekin.
5. Add salt and pepper.
6. Top with enough slices of brie to cover eggs.
7. Place in oven for 18–20 minutes (cheese will be brown and a knife inserted into ramekin will come out clean).

BROWN SUGAR CRUSTED MORNING MEATLOAF MAKES 4–6 SERVINGS

Transforming a traditional dinner into a breakfast dish is a great way to start the day. You can make this the night before and just pop it in the oven when it's time to put breakfast on the table.

1 minced ONION
1 clove GARLIC, minced
1 Tbsp. OLIVE OIL
½ lb. GROUND BEEF
½ lb. GROUND ITALIAN SAUSAGE
⅓ cup PLAIN PANKO CRUMBS
¼ tsp. DRIED THYME
1 (8-oz.) can TOMATO SAUCE
¼ cup BROWN SUGAR

1. Preheat oven to 375°F.
2. In a small frying pan over medium heat, combine onion, garlic, and oil until translucent. While onion and garlic are cooking, combine all remaining ingredients, except for brown sugar, in a mixing bowl. Add onions and garlic and mix well.
3. Press mixture into a 9-inch nonstick round pie pan. Sprinkle brown sugar liberally over meatloaf mix. Bake on top rack until cooked through (15 minutes).

EASY BACON AND SAGE FRITTATA MAKES 3–4 SERVINGS

Broiling your eggs creates a chewy cheese crust that covers your tender eggs. This wonderful texture contrast is a great way to start the day.

- 2 strips BACON
- 1/4 ONION, chopped
- 6 EGGS
- 2 tsp. WATER
- 1 1/2 tsp. FRESH SAGE, minced (or 1/2 tsp. dry rubbed sage)
- 1/2 tsp. SALT
- 1/4 tsp. BLACK PEPPER
- 1/4 cup SHREDDED CHEESE

1. Preheat oven to 350°F.
2. Put bacon and onion in a 9-inch nonstick round baking pan, and cook on top rack (5–10 minutes).
3. While bacon is cooking, combine eggs, water, sage, salt, and black pepper in a mixing bowl and whisk well.
4. Once bacon is done, remove from pan and dice into small chunks. Add onion and bacon to egg mixture.
5. Spray nonstick baking pan with cooking spray and add egg mixture to pan. Top with cheese.
6. Bake on medium rack for 15 minutes.

EASY POACHED EGGS MAKES 1 SERVING

Poached eggs can be scary. But adding vinegar to the water helps the egg set quickly, reducing the risk of turning your poached eggs into egg drop soup.

8 cups WATER
1/4 cup WHITE VINEGAR
2 GRADE AA EGGS
SALT AND PEPPER

1. In a 4-quart or larger saucepan, bring water and vinegar to a boil. Reduce heat until water is still bubbling, but bubbles don't break surface of water.
2. Gently crack 1 egg onto a small saucer that will easily fit into water.
3. Using a heat-safe spatula, stir water in a circular motion until a small whirlpool has formed.
4. Gently lower egg into whirlpool, taking care not to lower your hand in with it.
5. Repeat with other egg. (When making multiple servings, keep no more than 4 eggs in water at a time.)
6. Cook each egg for 3–5 minutes. Then remove with a slotted spoon.
7. Add salt and pepper to taste.

GRAPEFRUIT BRÛLÉE MAKES 2 SERVINGS

The classic breakfast of grapefruit with sprinkled sugar is transformed into a rich and decadent start to the morning. Broiling adds a ton of flavor, without adding calories.

1 **GRAPEFRUIT**, whole
2 Tbsp. **BROWN SUGAR**

1. Turn your oven to broil.
2. Slice just enough off the top and bottom of grapefruit that it lays flat (approximately ¼ inch off of each end). Slice grapefruit in half along the equator. Gently cut around each segment, but leave the segment within the grapefruit half.
3. Place both halves of grapefruit on a cookie sheet. Put 1 tablespoon of brown sugar on each half and spread brown sugar across top of fruit.
4. Place grapefruit immediately under broiler, and cook until sugar has dissolved and starts bubbling.

Appetizers

PUMPKIN CHEDDAR FONDUE SERVES 6–8

Pumpkin is loaded with vitamins and antioxidants, and pairs well with the savory cheese. Why not serve it year round?

1 cup PUMPKIN PUREE
1 cup STOCK OR BROTH
2 Tbsp. FLOUR
1 Tbsp. LEMON JUICE
8 oz. shredded SHARP CHEDDAR CHEESE
¼ tsp. NUTMEG
APPLES, PEARS, and CRUSTY BREAD

1. Combine pumpkin puree, stock, flour, and lemon juice. Mix until all lumps from flour have dissolved.
2. Place in a 2-quart or larger saucepan over medium to medium-high heat.
3. Add cheese and nutmeg. Cook until fondue thickens and cheese is fully melted.
4. Serve with apples, pears, and crusty bread.

DRY ROASTED GARLIC GARBANZO BEANS MAKES 4 SERVINGS

This recipe was developed as a way to serve nut-free snacks in an environment with food allergies. Who knew allergy-free living could taste this good?

1 (12-oz.) can GARBANZO BEANS (CHICKPEAS)
1 Tbsp. VEGETABLE OIL
½ tsp. GARLIC POWDER
½ tsp. SALT

1. Preheat your oven to 350°F.
2. Drain beans from can, rinse well, and drain again. Combine beans and vegetable oil and toss to combine.
3. Add garlic powder and salt to beans and mix well.
4. Place in a single layer on a cookie sheet and bake for 45–60 minutes, until beans are approximately half their size and are completely dry.
5. Let cool before enjoying.

GRILL ROASTED BABA GHANOUSH MAKES 8–10 SERVINGS

Grilling your eggplant gives it a rich, smoky flavor not normally found in baba ghanoush. This dip is rich, creamy, and sure to please.

1–2 EGGPLANTS (totaling 2 lb.)
¼ cup EXTRA-VIRGIN OLIVE OIL, divided
4 cloves GARLIC, with skin still on
juice from 1 LEMON
2 Tbsp. TAHINI (sesame seed paste)
SALT
chopped PARSLEY

1. Cut top and bottom from eggplant, and then cut in half. Slather cut side of eggplant with 2 tablespoons olive oil. Place cut side down on a grill over medium-low heat. Cook until eggplant is relatively soft and skin starts to peel away from flesh. Remove and let cool for 5–10 minutes.
2. While eggplant is cooking, place cloves of garlic on the coolest part of your grill and cook until tender. Remove, let cool, and remove skin.
3. Tailgate version: Scoop flesh of eggplant into a large bowl and combine with garlic. Mash with a fork until relatively pureed. Add lemon juice, tahini, and 2 tablespoons olive oil and mix well to combine. Add salt to taste.
4. Home version: Combine eggplant, garlic, lemon juice, tahini, and 2 tablespoons olive oil in a food processor, puree on pulse 8–9 times until smooth. Add salt to taste.
5. Finish off either version by sprinkling with chopped parsley and serving with pita chips.

CORN AND BLUEBERRY SALSA MAKES 8–10 SERVINGS

Grilling the corn intensifies its sweetness, bringing out the natural sugar in the blueberries. The avocado lends a creamy texture.

2 Tbsp. OLIVE OIL
4 ears of CORN, husked
1 JALAPEÑO PEPPER
¼ small RED ONION, minced
1 ripe AVOCADO
1 cup of FRESH BLUEBERRIES
juice from 1 LIME
¼ cup coarsely chopped CILANTRO LEAVES
SALT

1. Oil corn generously and place on a hot grill, turning every 5 minutes until cooked through (about 20 minutes total). Let cool. Then cut corn off of cobs using a sharp knife.
2. While corn is cooking, place jalapeño pepper on the grill and cook until skin starts to blister. Let cool, remove stem and seeds, and mince into small pieces.
3. Soak minced onion in cold water for 5–10 minutes and let drain.
4. Peel avocado and cut into ¼-inch chunks.
5. Combine all ingredients and mix well. Add salt to taste.

GRILLED WATERMELON PICO DE GALLO MAKES ENOUGH FOR 6 APPETIZERS

Replace the tomatoes with watermelon for a refreshing chip topping not normally associated with pico de gallo.

1 tsp. sliced RED ONION (approximately a whisper)
2 (½-inch thick) slices WATERMELON
1 CUCUMBER, peeled, seeded, and cut into small pieces
½ JALAPEÑO PEPPER, seeded and chopped into tiny pieces
2 Tbsp. chopped CILANTRO
juice from 1 LEMON
1 Tbsp. HONEY
SALT

1. Put slices of red onion in a bowl of water, and soak for 15–30 minutes. Drain and mince.
2. While onion is soaking, place watermelon slices directly on a hot grill and cook approximately 3 minutes per side. Let cool and cut into ¼-inch chunks.
3. Combine all ingredients and mix well.
4. Salt to taste.

APRICOTS WITH BALSAMIC MASCARPONE MAKES 2 SERVINGS

The sweetness of the apricots is perfectly balanced by the acidity in the mascarpone cheese. When combined with the saltiness of the pancetta, this appetizer is a great way to use summer apricots.

4 slices THINLY SLICED PANCETTA
3 Tbsp. fresh MASCARPONE CHEESE
1 tsp. BALSAMIC VINEGAR
1 Tbsp. HONEY
4 sliced APRICOTS

1. Over medium-low heat, cook pancetta until brown, remove from heat, and set on paper towel to remove grease.
2. In another container, combine mascarpone, vinegar, and honey. Mix well to combine.
3. Spread sliced apricots in a shallow and wide bowl. Form mascarpone mix into a small sphere and place in the middle of apricots. Crumble pancetta into small pieces and sprinkle over entire dish.

NOTE

» For more bite, try putting some finely chopped shallots on top of mascarpone.

BUTTERNUT SQUASH HUMMUS MAKES 4 SERVINGS

The rich orange color of this hummus is only matched by its velvety texture. Canned chickpeas can be used if you rinse and drain them well.

3 cups BUTTERNUT SQUASH, cut into ½-inch cubes
¼ cup OLIVE OIL, plus 1 Tbsp. to coat butternut squash
2 cloves GARLIC, sliced
1 cup COOKED CHICKPEAS (GARBANZO BEANS), drained
1 Tbsp. SEA SALT
½ tsp. CUMIN
¼ cup LEMON JUICE

1. Preheat oven to 375°F.
2. Lightly toss butternut squash in 1 tablespoon olive oil. Spread squash out in a baking sheet and cook until fork tender. Remove from oven and add to a food processor.
3. In a shallow frying pan, cook ¼ cup olive oil and garlic until garlic is fragrant but not brown.
4. Add oil/garlic mixture, chickpeas, salt, cumin, and lemon juice to butternut squash and puree.
5. Serve with Lots of Layers Flatbread and Chocolate Balsamic Reduction (on next page).

LOTS OF LAYERS FLATBREAD MAKES 6 PIECES OF FLATBREAD

The beauty of this flatbread is the folding method outlined below. The layers of dough are separated by layers of olive oil, creating an incredibly light and layered interior for the flatbread.

1 pkg. RAPID RISE YEAST (about 2¼ tsp.)
1 cup LUKEWARM WATER
2⅔ cups FLOUR
2 Tbsp. OLIVE OIL for dough, plus additional to top flatbread
1 Tbsp. SALT
KOSHER SALT

1. Preheat oven to 350°F.
2. Combine yeast and water and let sit for 10 minutes. Add flour, olive oil, and 1 tablespoon salt. Mix until a ball forms. Cover with a moist towel and let rest for 15–30 minutes. Divide dough into 6 even balls.
3. Roll 1 dough ball into a circle. Then spread a generous amount of oil across the top. Fold dough circle into thirds, as if you were folding a letter, applying oil on each exposed edge. Fold sides of "letter" into thirds again, applying oil.
4. Roll dough square out until it is approximately ⅛ inch thick. Repeat previous steps for remaining balls of dough. Sprinkle each flatbread with salt and bake for 10–15 minutes until top and bottom start to brown.

CHOCOLATE BALSAMIC REDUCTION MAKES ¼ CUP

Ordinarily chocolate and vinegar don't mix well, but by reducing the balsamic vinegar, it thickens just enough to create an emulsion with the melted chocolate. The result is a sauce with rich tree fruit notes, contrasted by a pleasing smokiness.

1 cup BALSAMIC VINEGAR
½ oz. UNSWEETENED CHOCOLATE, cut into small pieces

1. Cook vinegar over medium-low heat until steaming, but not boiling. Keep heat as low as possible to maintain as much flavor in vinegar as possible (boiling actually causes flavor to leave dish).
2. Reduce by ¾, leaving approximately ¼ cup of balsamic vinegar.
3. Over low heat, gently stir chocolate pieces into vinegar until completely melted.
4. Best served warm (drizzles better). If too thick, warm over gentle heat until possible to drizzle.

OLIVE ROASTED ALMONDS MAKES 8–10 SERVINGS

The trick to this dish is getting the almonds nice and brown before putting them in the oven. The heat of the pan browns the almonds, but it is too intense to dehydrate them. By using a two-step browning and roasting strategy, you get the intense flavor of the browning process with the light texture that comes from evaporating the moisture in the oven. This is a *great* appetizer that will go fast. Make extra.

2 Tbsp. OLIVE OIL
1 (3-inch) sprig ROSEMARY
8 oz. raw WHOLE ALMONDS
1 Tbsp SEA SALT
4 oz. assorted GREEK OLIVES IN RED WINE VINEGAR
¼ cup "OLIVE JUICE" (from Greek olives)

1. Preheat oven to 325°F.
2. Preheat olive oil in an oven-safe frying pan over medium or high heat until oil starts to shimmer.
3. Remove leaves from rosemary and place leaves in oil, tossing until all leaves are coated.
4. Reduce heat to medium. Add almonds and salt and toss in oil. Let roast for 10 minutes, stirring every 2 minutes (almonds will start to make a popping noise).
5. Add olives and olive juice to almonds.
6. Transfer entire mix to the oven and roast for 30 minutes, stirring every 10 minutes.
7. Remove from oven and serve while still warm.

NOTE

» Be sure to brown the almonds before putting them in the oven. The heat of the pan while on the stove causes all sorts of chemical reactions, creating some pretty great flavor compounds. However, if you were to keep the almonds on the stove, they would burn before the moisture in the middle was gone.

"SMOKED" KALE CHIPS MAKES 4 SERVINGS

Kale can be a challenge to eat, but when it's prepared this way, you won't be able to keep the bowl full.

1 bunch KALE
1 Tbsp. EXTRA-VIRGIN OLIVE OIL or SESAME OIL
1 Tbsp. FINE SEA SALT
1 tsp. SMOKED PAPRIKA

1. Wash kale thoroughly and let dry.
2. With a knife or kitchen scissors, remove thick stem from middle of each kale leaf. Tear remaining leaf into chip-size pieces.
3. Drizzle kale with olive oil, sea salt, and smoked paprika.
4. Load baking sheet with one layer of kale and cook in a 350°F oven for 10–15 minutes, or until edges are slightly brown.

LIME CHILI POPCORN MAKES 4 SERVINGS

Break beyond plain buttered popcorn with spices that intensify the flavor without adding calories.

16 cups POPPED POPCORN
1/4 cup MELTED BUTTER
zest and juice from 1 LIME
1 tsp. CHIPOTLE
SALT

1. Preheat the oven to 300°F. Line a baking sheet with foil.
2. Put the popcorn in a large, clean paper bag. In a medium-size bowl, whisk together the butter, lime zest, and lime juice.
3. Drizzle half of butter mixture over popcorn, fold over top of bag, and shake until popcorn is coated and moist. Add more butter mixture and give a second shake. Sprinkle chipotle over popcorn, and fold over top of bag. Shake a few times to coat.
4. Spread popcorn evenly over a baking sheet and bake until popcorn is dry, 5–7 minutes.
5. Salt to taste.

TRUFFLE PARMESAN POPCORN MAKES 4 SERVINGS

Most truffle oil on the market today is extra-virgin olive oil with natural truffle flavoring, but no actual truffles. If you can find oil that contains actual truffles, treat it like gold.

16 cups POPPED POPCORN
2 Tbsp. WHITE TRUFFLE OIL
1/4 cup grated PARMESAN CHEESE
SALT

1. Combine all ingredients and toss to incorporate. Salt to taste.

MAGIC FRY BATTER MAKES ENOUGH TO COAT 12–15 ITEMS, DEPENDING ON SIZE

Your favorite fried foods will never be so tasty. It's a crunchy batter with just a hint of sweetness.

1 cup FLOUR
½ cup CORNSTARCH
½ cup SUGAR
1 cup NONALCOHOLIC BEER
1 tsp. SALT

1. Combine all ingredients and dip favorite food in batter. Fry and serve.

NOTE

» Works well with: sandwich cookies, chicken tenders, mushrooms, and zucchini strips.

GRILLED ZUCCHINI ROLLS MAKES 4–6 SERVINGS (3 ROLLS EACH)

These appetizers are as tasty as they are good looking. The goat cheese gives each bite a feel of rich earthiness.

3–4 medium ZUCCHINIS
OLIVE OIL
1 RED PEPPER, roasted (see p. 104 for instructions)
1 (3.5-oz.) container GOAT CHEESE
1 Tbsp. fresh chopped BASIL (1 tsp. dried)
1½ tsp. BALSAMIC VINEGAR
¼ tsp. SALT

1. Slice zucchini lengthwise into ¼-inch thick strips. Discard end cuts. Lightly coat each piece of zucchini with olive oil. Place on a preheated grill and cook through, turning once.
2. While zucchini is cooking, combine goat cheese, basil, vinegar, and salt in a bowl, and mix well.
3. Slice roasted red pepper into ¼-inch thick wedges, just longer than your zucchini is wide.
4. Add ½–¾ tsp. goat cheese mixture to top of each zucchini strip and spread to coat.
5. Place 1 red pepper strip on one end of a zucchini strip, perpendicular to zucchini strip. Starting at end containing red pepper, roll zucchini strip into a roll. Chill before serving.

Side Dishes

PUMPKIN GNOCCHI WITH CITRUS BROWN BUTTER MAKES 4 SERVINGS

If you don't have enough time, get store-bought gnocchi in a pinch. Then just make the citrus brown butter as a topping.

The Gnocchi

1 (15-oz.) can PUMPKIN PUREE (not pumpkin pie filling)
3/4 cup DRY MASHED POTATO FLAKES
1/4 tsp. NUTMEG
1/4 tsp. CINNAMON
1 tsp. TABLE SALT
1 EGG
1 cup FLOUR, plus 1/4 cup for dusting as you roll the pasta

The Sauce

4 Tbsp. BUTTER
2 Tbsp. FRESH MINCED SAGE (or 2 tsp. dry rubbed sage)
juice from 1/2 LEMON (about 4 tsp.)
1/2 cup quartered MUSHROOMS

1. Fill a 6-quart or larger stockpot with water. Put pot on stove and heat on high.
2. While water is warming up, combine pumpkin, potato flakes, nutmeg, cinnamon, salt, and egg. Mix well.
3. Add flour to pumpkin mixture and mix until combined.
4. Split dough into 4 portions and roll out each portion into a long "worm," about ½-inch thick.
5. Cut worms into 1-inch lengths. Using the tines of a fork, gently drag fork tines across top of each 1-inch length, creating divots in gnocchi.
6. Meanwhile, start sauce by adding butter to a shallow frying pan over medium heat and cooking until butter bubbles and starts to brown.
7. Add gnocchi to boiling water.
8. Lower heat on butter to medium-low and add sage, lemon juice, and mushrooms. Cook until mushrooms are tender.
9. Once gnocchi starts to float in boiling water (3–4 minutes), remove.
10. Toss gnocchi with citrus butter sauce and enjoy!

HERBED SPAETZLE MAKES 4 SERVINGS

Although the pronunciation is open to controversy (some say SPAY-tzle, others say SCHPETZ-lah, there's no controversy about the flavor.

The Spaetzle

1 cup FLOUR
1 tsp. SALT
½ tsp. GROUND NUTMEG
1 pinch PEPPER
¼ cup MILK
2 EGGS
4 tsp. FRESH HERBS, chopped (parsley, rosemary, and sage work well)

The Topping

4 Tbsp. BUTTER, divided
1 Tbsp. EXTRA-VIRGIN OLIVE OIL
8 oz. sliced MUSHROOMS
1 diced YELLOW ONION
4 tsp. FRESH HERBS (same kind as above)
SALT AND PEPPER

1. Bring a large pot of water to boil (5-quart stockpot or bigger).
2. Combine flour, salt, nutmeg, and pepper, mixing to combine.
3. Add milk and eggs. Mix together until a soft batter is formed. Add herbs.
4. Separate batter into 3 batches. Using a large mixing spoon with holes in its bottom as your press, place and press batter through holes directly into boiling water. Continue until all batter is gone. Spaetzle is done when it starts to float to the surface of the water (about 2 minutes per batch). Remove each batch of spaetzle from boiling water and set aside before starting next batch.
5. Once spaetzle is completed, add 2 tablespoons butter and olive oil to a large stockpot and melt. Add mushrooms and cook until mushrooms start to soften (3–4 minutes). Add onion and cook until translucent.
6. Add remaining 2 tablespoons butter and spaetzle to butter and onion mixture and cook for 1–2 minutes. Add fresh herbs, salt and pepper to taste, and serve!

LEMON CAPER BRUSSELS SPROUTS MAKES 4 SERVINGS

Lemon, parmesan, and butter—even the most ardent brussels sprouts foes will want to dive into this dish.

1 lb. BRUSSELS SPROUTS
3 Tbsp. OLIVE OIL
2 Tbsp. BUTTER
2 Tbsp. NONPAREIL CAPERS
juice from ½ a LEMON (1 Tbsp.)
¼ cup grated PARMESAN
SALT

1. Rinse all sprouts and remove outer leaves. Cut into halves.
2. In a large sauté pan, preheat olive oil over medium heat. Add brussels sprouts and cook until sprouts start to brown, stirring occasionally.
3. Once brown, add butter and remove from heat when melted. Add capers and lemon juice. Garnish with parmesan. Add salt to taste.

BRAISED KALE MAKES 4 SERVINGS

Removing the coarse stem from kale leaves allows for a quick cooking time. The easiest way to cut the stem out is to fold the kale leaf in half at the stem and run your knife between the stem and leaf.

1 Tbsp. OLIVE OIL
1 yellow ONION, diced
1 clove GARLIC, minced
¼ cup minced MUSHROOMS
4 cups KALE, middle stem removed and chopped into bite-size pieces
¼ cup LIQUID (chicken stock or white wine preferred)
juice from 1 LEMON
½ tsp. CHILI FLAKES
¼ tsp. TOASTED SESAME OIL
SALT to taste

1. In a large sauté pan add oil, onion, garlic, and mushroom, and cook over medium-high heat until onions and garlic start to brown. Then add kale, liquid, lemon, chili flakes, sesame oil, and salt. Stir.
2. Reduce heat to medium and cover. Cook for 8–10 minutes, or until kale is tender.

PUMPKIN QUINOA MAKES 4 SERVINGS

Although thought of as a grain, quinoa is actually a seed grown in the high altitudes of the Andes mountains. Make sure the quinoa you purchase is prerinsed to remove the bitter saponins.

- 2 cups DRY QUINOA
- 2 cups CHICKEN STOCK (or reconstituted chicken bouillon)
- 2 cups WATER
- 1/2 cup PUMPKIN PUREE
- 1/2 tsp. TABLE SALT
- 1/4 tsp. NUTMEG
- 1/4 tsp. CARDAMOM
- 2 Tbsp. PARMESAN CHEESE

1. Add all ingredients except parmesan to a 4-quart saucepan and heat over medium heat.
2. Cook until quinoa absorbs all moisture, stirring occasionally to prevent dish from sticking to bottom of pan.
3. Garnish with parmesan cheese before serving.

PUMPKIN RISOTTO MAKES 4 SERVINGS

A pumpkin dish that allows the pumpkin to shine. Full of flavor, sweet, savory, and rich.

2 Tbsp. EXTRA-VIRGIN OLIVE OIL
5 WHOLE SAGE LEAVES (optional)
1 minced SHALLOT
1 Tbsp. minced FRESH GINGER (or 1 tsp. dried/powdered)
1 cup ARBORIO RICE
2 cups unsalted chicken or vegetable STOCK.
½ cup CARROT JUICE
½ cup PUMPKIN PUREE
½ cup PARMESAN CHEESE
1 Tbsp. APPLE CIDER VINEGAR
½ tsp. DRIED SAGE
SALT

1. In a 2-quart or larger saucepan, preheat olive oil over medium to medium-high heat.
2. Optional—Add sage leaves and cook for 30–60 seconds. Remove and set on a paper towel to dry.
3. Add shallot and ginger. Let cook until just translucent (60–90 seconds).
4. Add rice and stir until coated with olive oil. Continue stirring until rice turns from translucent to solid white.
5. Combine stock and carrot juice. Add just enough stock mixture to cover the rice (should be no more than ¼ of the total liquid). Stir frequently.
6. Continue the process of adding liquid, making sure liquid never rises above level of rice. Continue to stir frequently.
7. Cook until rice is al dente (roughly 45 minutes).
8. Add pumpkin, vinegar, parmesan cheese, and dried sage. Stir until cheese is melted. Salt to taste.
9. Serve immediately and garnish with fried sage leaves.

BRAISED SUMMER SQUASH MAKES 4 SERVINGS

The old wisdom "Never leave your car unlocked at church, because you'll end up with a vehicle full of zucchini" has an element of truth to it. Cooking your summer squash this way creates a decadent side dish full of freshness.

2 finely diced APPLES
2 cups cubed ZUCCHINI
2 cups cubed YELLOW SQUASH
1 diced ONION
1 cup chicken or vegetable STOCK
2 Tbsp. MAPLE SYRUP
½ tsp. CINNAMON
1 (6-inch) sprig ROSEMARY (or 1 Tbsp. dry)
SALT

1. Preheat oven to 350°F.
2. Combine apples, zucchini, squash, and onion in a 9 x 13 pan. Add vegetable stock, maple syrup, and cinnamon. Toss to combine.
3. Place rosemary sprig so that it rests in the stock.
4. Cover with aluminum foil and bake for 25–30 minutes.
5. Salt to taste and remove rosemary sprig before serving.

CANDIED BRUSSELS SPROUTS MAKES 4 SERVINGS

Brussels sprouts are one of my favorite vegetables. This once frequently maligned (and overcooked) vegetable can be transformed into a decadent side dish with just a little love.

4 Tbsp. BUTTER
1 tsp. LEMON JUICE
½ tsp. SALT
1 medium YELLOW ONION, chopped
¼ cup BROWN SUGAR
1–1½ lb. BRUSSELS SPROUTS

1. In an 8-inch or larger frying pan add butter, lemon juice, salt, and onion.
2. Cook over medium-high heat until onion is translucent.
3. Add brown sugar and mix it in. Increase heat to high and cook until mixture starts bubbling rapidly (1–2 minutes).
4. Reduce heat to medium, add brussels sprouts, and stir occasionally until sprouts are cooked through (4–5 minutes).

SAGE AND BROWN BUTTER MASHED POTATOES MAKES 10–15 SERVINGS

Rinsing your potatoes after boiling them removes a layer of starch (called "amylose") that can cause the mashed potatoes to be gummy.

10–12 MEDIUM RUSSET POTATOES
½ cup BUTTER
10–15 WHOLE SAGE LEAVES
1 cup MILK
SALT

1. Peel potatoes and boil in a tall stockpot with salted water until fork tender. Move to a colander and rinse for 10–15 seconds.
2. Empty stockpot and add butter. Cook over medium heat until butter starts to darken. Add sage leaves and fry for 15–20 seconds. Remove sage and set on paper towel to dry. Reduce heat on stove to prevent butter from burning.
3. Carefully add milk to butter. Butter will be hot and will splash, so watch for errant butter flares!
4. Put individual potatoes through a potato ricer and add to butter and milk mixture.
5. Mince fried sage leaves and add to potatoes. Mix well and salt to taste.

ZUCCHINI WITH PINE NUTS MAKES 4 SERVINGS

Toasting the pine nuts unlocks a fragrant richness that pairs well with the rosemary and zucchini. When topped with smoked salt it creates a vegetarian side dish that pairs well with the heartiest of main courses.

3 Tbsp. EXTRA-VIRGIN OLIVE OIL
¼ tsp. PINE NUTS
2 Tbsp. chopped FRESH ROSEMARY (or 2 tsp. dry)
1 medium YELLOW ONION, diced
1 large ZUCCHINI, seeded, peeled, and cut into bite size chunks
1 YELLOW CROOKNECK SQUASH, cut into bite size chunks
2 tsp. SMOKED SALT
½ cup CHICKEN STOCK

1. In a large sauté pan add olive oil, pine nuts, and rosemary over medium heat. Cook until rosemary starts to smell fragrant.
2. Add onion to pan and cook until translucent.
3. Add zucchini, crookneck squash, smoked salt, and chicken stock to pan and cover.
4. Reduce to medium-low heat and cook until squash is completely cooked through.

KALAMATA LENTILS MAKES 6 SERVINGS

Lentils can be tricky to work with as they tend to split easily. The trick: don't bring them to a boil. If you can keep your water in the 170–180 degree range you'll get almost no lentil split.

16 oz. dried LENTILS
1 minced SHALLOT
2 cloves GARLIC, minced
5 peeled and chopped CARROTS
1 TOMATO, diced
2 LEEKS, dark green portions discarded and chopped into ½-inch sections
2 big handfuls FRESH SPINACH
½ cup KALAMATA OLIVES, roughly chopped
1 Tbsp. minced FRESH ROSEMARY
SALT to taste

1. Cook lentils at optimal temperature in at least 8 cups of water. Cook until tender.
2. While lentils are cooking, add shallot and garlic to a large frying pan, and cook until translucent. Add carrots, tomato, and leeks, stirring occasionally for 4–5 minutes.
3. Add spinach to veggies and stir. Cover and cook for 5 minutes, stirring once or twice.
4. Once lentils are cooked, drain water. Add all cooked veggies to lentils. Add olives, rosemary, and salt.
5. Stir and enjoy!

HAZELNUT BRUSSELS SPROUTS MAKES 6 SERVINGS

Brussels sprouts have gotten a bad rap over the years, usually because they're cooked much longer than Mother Nature ever intended. A quick roast in the oven brings out their natural sweetness, and keeps them full of life.

- 2 lb. BRUSSELS SPROUTS
- 2 Tbsp. EXTRA-VIRGIN OLIVE OIL
- SALT to taste
- 1/2 cup HAZELNUTS, peeled and coarsely chopped
- 1/4 cup APPLE CIDER VINEGAR
- 2 Tbsp. WHITE TRUFFLE OIL

1. Preheat oven to 350°F.
2. Clean and trim brussels sprouts. Carefully cut each individual sprout into 4 segments (chiffonade). Toss with olive oil and salt. Put one layer of sprouts on a sheet pan and bake for 20–30 minutes (until sprouts start to brown). (You may need more than one sheet pan.)
3. When brussels sprouts have 10 minutes remaining, add hazelnuts to oven in a separate pan.
4. Once done cooking, combine brussels sprouts and hazelnuts in a bowl. Drizzle with vinegar and truffle oil. Toss and serve.

COCONUT LIME RISOTTO MAKES 4 SERVINGS

The trick to good risotto—you put in the lime and the coconut and stir it all up. And stir some more, and some more. The stirring action releases the pent up starch inside the rice that ultimately creates the trademark creamy texture. Your stirring will be rewarded with an amazing rice dish.

- 1 Tbsp. OLIVE OIL
- ½ medium YELLOW ONION, minced
- 1 clove GARLIC, minced
- 1 cup ARBORIO RICE
- 1 (12-oz.) can COCONUT MILK
- CHICKEN STOCK to make 2½ cups total liquid (about 1 cup)
- Juice from 1 LIME
- SALT
- grated NUTMEG for garnishing

1. Combine oil, onion, and garlic in a 2-quart or larger saucepan over medium-high heat, cooking until onion is translucent (but not brown). Add rice and stir, stir, stir until rice turns from clear to white (microscopic cracks form in rice, releasing starch and causing individual grains to reflect light, making grain turn a solid color).
2. Combine coconut milk, lime juice, and chicken stock. Add just enough liquid to cover rice (should be no more than ¼ of total liquid). Stir frequently.
3. Continue process of adding liquid, making sure liquid never rises above level of rice. Stir frequently.
4. Cook until rice is al dente (roughly 45 minutes). Salt to taste.
5. Garnish with some grated nutmeg.

SPINACH AND CANNELLINIS MAKES 4 SERVINGS

Smoked salt can usually be found near the deli of your supermarket. Look for applewood smoked salt because it gives the flavor of bacon, without the calories or saturated fat.

3 Tbsp. EXTRA-VIRGIN OLIVE OIL
1 (12-oz.) pack WHOLE CRIMINI MUSHROOMS, washed and cut into fourths (sometimes called baby bellas).
1 minced YELLOW ONION
1 (16-oz.) can CANNELLINI BEANS, drained and rinsed
1 lb. FRESH SPINACH
juice from 1 LEMON (about 2 Tbsp.)
½ teaspoon SMOKED SALT (optional)
SALT

1. Preheat a large sauté pan over medium heat and add olive oil.
2. Add mushrooms and cook until mushrooms are brown and start to shrink in size (about 5 minutes).
3. Add onion and cook until translucent (3–4 minutes). Add cannellini beans and stir gently.
4. Top mixture with spinach, lemon juice, and smoked salt; and cover with pan lid.
5. Reduce to medium-low heat and cook until spinach wilts and shrinks (about 5 minutes).
6. Add additional salt to taste.

HOMEMADE KETCHUP MAKES APPROXIMATELY 2 CUPS

As fall approaches and gardens ripen, there is an amazing opportunity to take advantage of the warm and inviting taste of homemade ketchup. For 335 days a year, I prefer the kind from the bottle. But for a brief period every year, when tomatoes are at their peak, nothing compares to a fresh batch of homemade ketchup.

3 lb. FRESH TOMATOES (plum-type tomatoes preferred), peeled and deseeded
1/2 YELLOW ONION, diced
2 cloves GARLIC, peeled
1/4 cup CIDER VINEGAR
1/4 cup AGAVE NECTAR (or substitute 1/3 cup brown sugar if agave is unavailable)
SALT

1. Combine tomatoes, onion, and garlic in a saucepan over very low heat. Let it cook for 15 minutes, stirring occasionally.
2. Add vinegar and agave. Let it continue to cook for another 45 minutes, stirring occasionally.
3. Puree using a food processor or immersion blender. Salt to taste and enjoy.
4. Keep refrigerated.

VARIATIONS

» Add 1 to 2 finely minced chipotle peppers for a nice kick.

» Add 1 peach with tomatoes for a floral or sweet flavor.

CRÈME BRÛLÉE SWEET POTATOES MAKES 3–4 SERVINGS

This is a great way to eat sweet potatoes. If you have a mandoline, it makes slicing the sweet potatoes much easier.

2 medium SWEET POTATOES (or YAMS)
1 Tbsp. EXTRA-VIRGIN OLIVE OIL
¼ cup SUGAR
SOUR CREAM or GREEK YOGURT
SMOKED PAPRIKA or CHIPOTLE PEPPER

1. Preheat oven to 350°F.
2. Peel sweet potatoes and slice lengthwise about ⅛ inch thick (slice the opposite way of a potato chip).
3. Toss in oil, put in a single layer on a baking sheet, and cook until tender (15–20 minutes).
4. Sprinkle tops of the sweet potatoes with sugar.
5. Using either the broiler in your oven or a blowtorch, brûlée sugar until liquid and brown.
6. Arrange sweet potatoes as if they were peacock feathers, and add a dollop of sour cream or yogurt at the point of the fan.
7. Garnish with a light dusting of smoked paprika or chipotle and serve.

SWEET POTATO TATER TOTS MAKES 6 SERVINGS

By far one of the most fun recipes to make. Involve the little ones in the mixing and tater tot forming. Then let them stand back as you fry these delicious treats.

3–4 medium YAMS or SWEET POTATOES (enough to get 3 cups of shreds)
¼ cup FLOUR
¼ cup PARMESAN CHEESE
1 tsp. SALT
OIL for frying

1. Bring a large pot of water to a boil. Add yams or sweet potatoes with peels still on and boil for 20 minutes. Transfer out of water and let cool.
2. Peel potatoes. Using either a box grater or shredding attachment on a food processor, shred enough sweet potatoes to get 3 cups of shreds.
3. Place 4 sheets of paper towels on your countertop, dump shreds on paper towels, and fold towels up over shreds.
4. Push on shreds until you have squeezed as much moisture out as possible. Combine shreds with flour, cheese, and salt. Mix well to combine.
5. Using a tablespoon, portion out tater tots and form into small tater logs.
6. Fry in 350°F oil for 3–5 minutes, until brown.

ROASTED BUTTERNUT SQUASH WITH A COCOA NIB VINAIGRETTE MAKES 6–8 SERVINGS

Most stores sell precut butternut squash, and it's a great time-saver for this delicious recipe!

4 lb. BUTTERNUT SQUASH, peeled and cut into ¾-inch cubes
4 oz. PANCETTA, thinly sliced
1 finely MINCED SHALLOT
1 cup BALSAMIC VINEGAR, reduced to ¼ cup
2 Tbsp. COCOA NIBS
1 Tbsp. HONEY
¼ cup ROSEMARY/GARLIC INFUSED OLIVE OIL (see recipe below)
SALT

1. Preheat oven to 350°F.
2. Put squash in an oven-safe pan, and roast uncovered in oven until a knife inserted into squash goes in easily.
3. Fry pancetta a few pieces at a time in a frying pan until all pieces are crispy. Set aside on a paper towel to drain, and leave pancetta drippings in the pan. Add shallot to pancetta drippings, and cook until tender.
4. Add cooked shallot, balsamic vinegar reduction, cocoa nibs, and honey to a food processor. While food processor is running, slowly drizzle olive oil into the processor. Add salt to taste.
5. Top squash with crumbled pancetta and cocoa nib vinaigrette.
6. You may have some vinaigrette left over. Feel free to throw it on a salad; it's absolutely delicious.

ROSEMARY/GARLIC INFUSED OLIVE OIL MAKES 3/4 CUP

Once this is made, it needs to be stored in the refrigerator. If it lasts that long.

3/4 cup OLIVE OIL
1 (6-inch) stalk of FRESH ROSEMARY, cut into 1-inch segments
3 cloves peeled GARLIC

1. Add all ingredients to an oven safe vessel, narrow enough to submerge garlic and rosemary in olive oil. Place in a 200°F oven for approximately one hour. (I use a tall/narrow measuring cup).
2. Remove from oven, leave rosemary and garlic in oil, and cover. Let cool before using and store any extra in the refrigerator.

Soups and Salads

MAPLE BACON VINAIGRETTE MAKES 2/3 CUP

A delicious way to incorporate truly American flavors to your salad—bacon and maple.

3 oz. BACON
1 minced SHALLOT
2 Tbsp. APPLE CIDER VINEGAR
1/4 cup + 2 Tbsp. MAPLE SYRUP
1 Tbsp. BROWN SUGAR
1/4 cup EXTRA-VIRGIN OLIVE OIL
1/4 cup BACON DRIPPINGS, reserved from frying bacon
SALT

1. Pan fry bacon until crispy, remove bacon from pan, and pour drippings into a heat-safe measuring cup. Reserve enough bacon drippings in pan to cook shallot.
2. Add shallot to pan with drippings and cook over medium heat until translucent.
3. In a food processor or blender, combine shallots, vinegar, maple syrup, and brown sugar. Blend on high speed until ingredients are incorporated.
4. Combine olive oil and bacon drippings (be careful, drippings will still be hot).
5. *Slowly* drizzle oil/drippings mixture into your food processor. It should take 90–120 seconds to add everything.
6. While food processor/blender is still running, add 2/3 of cooked bacon. Save remaining bacon for garnishing your salad.
7. Stop food processor/blender and salt to taste.

GARLIC AND HERB VINAIGRETTE MAKES 2/3 CUP

Greek herbs are combined with Continental flavors for a salad dressing fusion that packs a punch.

1/4 cup LEMON JUICE
1 clove GARLIC
1/4 cup RED WINE VINEGAR
1 Tbsp. chopped FRESH OREGANO (or 1 tsp. dry)
1 Tbsp. chopped FRESH ROSEMARY (or 1 tsp. dry)
1/4–1/2 cup EXPELLER PRESSED PEANUT OIL

1. Combine lemon juice, garlic, vinegar, oregano, and rosemary in a food processor. Run processor until spices are chopped into relatively small pieces.
2. *Slowly* drizzle in oil while food processor is running. Start with teeny tiny amounts at first. Then continue to drizzle until all is added. (It should take 1–2 minutes to add oil if you're adding it slow enough.)

RASPBERRY LIME VINAIGRETTE MAKES 1 CUP

Summer flavors are captured in this delicious recipe perfect for an outdoor picnic.

1 cup WHOLE RASPBERRIES
1/4 cup RASPBERRY INFUSED VINEGAR
1 tsp. HONEY
1/4 cup SUGAR
juice from 1 LIME
1/4 cup NEUTRAL-FLAVORED OIL (like grape seed or canola oil)
SALT to taste

1. Combine raspberries, vinegar, honey, sugar, and lime juice in a blender/food processor. Mix until raspberries are pureed and all ingredients are incorporated.
2. Slowly drizzle in oil while the blender/food processor is running. Stop the blender/food processor and add salt.

ISRAELI COUSCOUS AND PEACH SALAD MAKES 4–6 SERVINGS

Israeli Couscous is slightly larger than the traditional variety and absorbs the flavors of the other ingredients, creating a fresh salad guaranteed to please.

1 cup ISRAELI COUSCOUS
½ YELLOW ONION, finely chopped
1 Tbsp. HONEY
1 Tbsp. APPLE CIDER VINEGAR
pinch of NUTMEG
2 Tbsp. EXTRA-VIRGIN OLIVE OIL
¼ cup TOASTED ALMOND SLIVERS
1 finely CHOPPED PEACH
SALT
4 medium FRESH BASIL LEAVES, cut into thin strips

1. Bring 3 quarts of water to a boil, add couscous, and cook until al dente (about 6 minutes). Strain and set cooked couscous aside.
2. In a small frying pan, cook onion until translucent.
3. Remove from heat and add honey, vinegar, nutmeg, olive oil, and almond slivers.
4. In a medium-size bowl combine all ingredients. Add salt to taste and garnish with fresh basil.

PEACH PANZANELLA MAKES 5–6 SERVINGS

Few things in life compare to a fresh peach picked during the height of the day. It's warm, luscious, and filled with flavor. Adding that perfect peach to this salad only enhances the flavor.

The Salad

4 cups **DENSE BREAD**, cubed into bite-size pieces (I prefer sourdough or french bread)
1/4 cup **EXTRA-VIRGIN OLIVE OIL** (California Olive Ranch brand is preferred)
1/2 tsp. **SALT**
4 **ROMA TOMATOES**, sliced
3–4 large **PEACHES**, sliced
10–15 **BASIL LEAVES**, cut into small strips
5 oz. **ARUGULA** (roughly 6 cups)

The Dressing

1/4 cup **EXTRA-VIRGIN OLIVE OIL**
1/4 cup **BALSAMIC VINEGAR**

1. In a large frying pan over medium heat, add olive oil. Let oil warm for 60 seconds, and then add bread, mixing rapidly to coat bread with olive oil. Sprinkle salt evenly over bread cubes. Cook for 5–10 minutes, stirring frequently until bread is golden brown.
2. While bread is toasting, add tomatoes, peaches, basil, and arugula to a large salad bowl.
3. In a small container, make a dressing by combining olive oil and balsamic vinegar. Mix well.
4. Add toasted bread to salad and toss gently to combine. Add dressing and toss again. Refrigerate for 15–30 minutes prior to serving to allow the bread to absorb moisture.

NOTE

» For added richness, after toasting bread, use the same pan over medium-low heat to gently warm peaches. Let cook for 10 minutes, stirring gently every 2–3 minutes.

BUFFALO POTATO SALAD MAKES 6–8 SERVINGS

This update to the traditional dish brings a new perspective that pairs well with game day activities.

2–2½ lb. small RED POTATOES
½ RED ONION, diced.
zest from 1 LEMON
2 Tbsp. EXTRA-VIRGIN OLIVE OIL
2 stalks CELERY, washed and chopped into bite-size pieces
¼ cup BUFFALO WING SAUCE (Frank's is preferred)
¼ cup chopped FRESH PARSLEY, (or 2 Tbsp. dried parsley flakes)
½ cup BLUE CHEESE CRUMBLES
SALT to taste

1. Wash potatoes and put in a large stockpot. Cover with water and bring to a boil. Cook until a knife or fork easily pierces potato (about 30 minutes). Strain and put in fridge until potatoes are cool.
2. Meanwhile, combine red onion, lemon zest, and olive oil in a frying pan over medium low heat. Cook until onion is translucent (5–10 minutes). Let cool.
3. Once potatoes are cool, slice into bite-size pieces and add to a large mixing bowl. Add onions/oil/lemon mixture, celery, Buffalo wing sauce, parsley, ½ of blue cheese, and salt. Mix well.
4. Before serving, sprinkle blue cheese crumbles on top as a garnish.

MEDITERRANEAN POTATO SALAD MAKES 6–8 SERVINGS

This potato salad takes the flavors of a Lebanese tabouli and combines it with a distinctly American dish.

3 lb. RED AND PURPLE POTATOES
1 medium YELLOW ONION
1 Tbsp. EXTRA-VIRGIN OLIVE OIL, for sautéing
½ cup minced FRESH PARSLEY
¼ cup minced FRESH MINT
¼ cup LEMON JUICE
¼ cup EXTRA-VIRGIN OLIVE OIL
SALT AND PEPPER to taste
½ tsp. CITRIC ACID (optional)

1. Clean all potatoes and place in a large stockpot. Cover potatoes with water, bring to a boil, and cook until a fork inserted into potato goes to the middle with minimal effort.
2. While potatoes are cooking, mince yellow onion and sauté over medium heat with olive oil. Cook until translucent.
3. Once potatoes and onion are cooked, cool ingredients down. Once cool, slice potatoes into bite-size pieces.
4. Combine parsley, mint, lemon juice, olive oil, salt and pepper, and citric acid. Mix into a dressing well.
5. Combine all ingredients, and gently toss to combine.

EASY PEASY CAPRESE MAKES 4–6 SERVINGS

Tomatoes picked at the height of freshness are the key to this deliciously simple salad. Try heirloom varieties like Brandywine or Purple Cherokee.

2 large, fresh picked **TOMATOES**
1/4 lb. **FRESH MOZZARELLA** (get Mozzarella di Bufala Campana if possible, but cow's milk mozzarella works well too)
4 **BASIL LEAVES**, cut into long thin strips (chiffonade)
1/2 cup **BALSAMIC VINEGAR**, reduced over low heat by 3/4 and chilled to room temperature
1 Tbsp. **EXTRA-VIRGIN OLIVE OIL**
COARSE SEA SALT to taste
CRACKED BLACK PEPPER to taste

1. Wash and chop tomatoes into bite-size pieces. Cut mozzarella into small bite-size chunks.
2. Combine tomatoes, mozzarella, and basil, reserving a few basil strips for garnish.
3. Coat with balsamic reduction and drizzle olive oil over salad.
4. Sprinkle salt and fresh cracked black pepper. Garnish with remaining basil strips.

NOTE

» Although a traditional caprese salad doesn't include balsamic vinegar, it really helps call out the sweetness in the fresh tomatoes.

» If you don't have fresh mozzarella, you can always use ricotta. I like to create a bed of arugala lettuce, top with tomatoes, and then add the ricotta, balsamic vinegar, basil, and olive oil.

» Tomatoes are *full* of lycopene, an oil soluble antioxidant. Studies have shown that a small amount of oil with tomatoes makes the lycopene much easier for your body to absorb.

BABY KALE SALAD WITH AVOCADO VINAIGRETTE MAKES 4–6 SERVINGS

As kale gets bigger so does its coarseness. By getting the younger variety, you'll get a more delicate leaf that still holds up to the strong flavors of basil, fennel, and grapefruit.

The Salad

10–12 oz. BABY KALE
1 MANGO, cut into small chunks
4–5 FRESH BASIL LEAVES, cut into thin strips
1 FENNEL BULB, shaved into small strips
2 GRAPEFRUITS, segmented

The Dressing

1 Tbsp. OLIVE OIL
2 cloves GARLIC
1 AVOCADO
¼ cup LEMON JUICE
1 tsp. SALT
extra OLIVE OIL for consistency

1. In a large bowl combine kale, mango, basil, fennel, and grapefruit segments.
2. Preheat olive oil in a shallow frying pan over medium-low heat. Add garlic and cook for 5–10 minutes.
3. Slice open avocado and remove pit. Scoop out flesh from inside of avocado into a blender/food processor. Add garlic/olive oil mixture, lemon juice, and salt. Process until smooth. You may need to add additional olive oil to get a smooth texture. The dressing will be thick.
4. Add dressing to salad and toss to combine.

MINT CUCUMBER SOUP MAKES 3–4 SERVINGS

Cantaloupe and cucumbers are considered by many eastern philosophies to be "cooling" food, meaning it should be eaten when the weather is hot to cool the body. Adding mint further enhances the cooling sensation and rounds out the dish.

1 CANTALOUPE, peeled, seeded, and cut into small pieces
juice from 2 LIMES
1 tsp. SALT
½ tsp. CHIPOTLE POWDER or SMOKED PAPRIKA
7–8 MINT LEAVES
1 CUCUMBER, peeled, seeded, and cut into small pieces
⅓ lb. STRAWBERRIES, stemmed and chopped

1. In a blender/food processor, add cantaloupe, lime juice, salt, chipotle/paprika, and mint. Process until completely pureed. Depending on the size of your blender, you may need to do this in shifts.
2. Strain cantaloupe puree through a medium mesh sieve into a large bowl.
3. Add cucumbers and strawberries. Mix well.
4. Garnish with mint and a strawberry slice. Enjoy!

HOMEMADE NOODLES MAKES ENOUGH FOR 2–3 QUARTS OF SOUP

One of my first memories of cooking was rolling noodles my mom had handmade for chicken noodle soup. Don't worry if the noodles aren't consistent, their beauty is in their variety.

1 tsp. SALT
1¼ cup FLOUR
2 EGGS
⅓ cup WATER

1. Combine salt, flour, and eggs in a mixer. Mix well. Once all ingredients except water are incorporated, add water a little bit at a time until dough ball is slightly tacky. You may end up using less water than recipe calls for. If you add too much water, add flour, ¼ cup at a time until dough feels just tacky.
2. Let dough rest for 15 minutes, and then dump onto a floured surface. Roll out into a long piece, about ⅛ inch thick.
3. If you have a pasta roller, make dough into ¼-inch wide noodles, and then cut into 2-inch lengths before adding to soup.
4. If you don't have a pasta roller, slice noodles by hand, taking care to maintain an even width.

SAVORY PARMESAN TUILES MAKES 8 SERVINGS

Adding a Parmesan Tuile to the top of a meat-based soup helps amplify the natural savor of the dish without adding a lot of salt.

PARCHMENT PAPER to cover a cookie sheet (or a nonstick baking sheet)
2 cups SHREDDED FRESH PARMESAN

1. Preheat oven to 350°F.
2. Separate cheese into 8 individual portions. Place parchment paper over top of a cookie sheet. Carefully place 8 portions of cheese on the parchment paper, with at least 2 inches between each pile of cheese.
3. Bake until cheese is melted and crispy (8–12 minutes).
4. Serve on top of salads or soups.

THE MOST AMAZING CHICKEN NOODLE SOUP YOU'LL EVER EAT

MAKES 8–10 SERVINGS

Chicken noodle soup is all about love. Anchovy paste contains the natural substance inosinate that amplifies the natural savor of the chicken by a factor of 20. The result: a rich, earth soup with a little bit of bite.

OIL for stockpot
1 packet UNFLAVORED GELATIN
1 lb. BONELESS/SKINLESS CHICKEN, cut into ¾-inch or smaller cubes
1 medium YELLOW ONION, diced into small chunks
½ inch GINGER ROOT, minced
2 minced GARLIC CLOVES
½ cup diced CRIMINI MUSHROOMS (also known as baby bellas)
2 cups diced CELERY
3 peeled WHOLE CARROTS, chopped
1 LEEK, sliced into circles and rinsed (Leeks tend to carry a LOT of dirt, so rinsing after chopping is crucial.)
8 cups CHICKEN STOCK (or use water and chicken meat base)
HOMEMADE NOODLES (see opposite), store-bought noodles can be substituted
1 packet MISO SOUP POWDER
1 tsp. ANCHOVY PASTE
FRESH GROUND BLACK PEPPER
SALT
1 bunch CILANTRO, minced
up to 2 qt. additional WATER as necessary

1. Place a 6-quart stockpot over high heat and add just enough oil to coat bottom of pan. Add unflavored gelatin to ½ cup cold water in a separate dish and let sit for 10 minutes. Stir gelatin to make sure no lumps have formed. Add chicken to oil and fry until exterior of chicken starts to brown. Add onions, ginger, garlic, and mushrooms and continue to fry until onions are translucent. Add celery, carrots, and leek. Cook until veggies start to sweat. Add chicken stock, bring to a boil, and then reduce heat to a simmer. Add unflavored gelatin.
2. Add noodles. Cook until noodles are tender. Add miso soup powder and anchovy paste. Mix well. Add additional water as necessary to keep the soup "soupy." Add black pepper and salt to taste.
3. 1–2 minutes prior to serving, add cilantro and stir well.
4. Garnish with Parmesan Tuiles (see opposite).

WATERMELON GAZPACHO MAKES 4–6 SERVINGS

Adding watermelon to gazpacho transforms it into a light and fresh summertime soup. Soaking the onions prior to serving mutes their harshness but leaves their sweetness.

1 tsp. RED ONION (approximately a whisper)
2 cups chopped SEEDLESS WATERMELON
1 TOMATO, seeds removed
½ RED BELL PEPPER, pith removed
1 JALAPEÑO, seeds and pith removed (optional)
zest from 1 SMALL LIME
juice from 2 SMALL LIMES (about ¼ cup)
2 Tbsp. EXTRA-VIRGIN OLIVE OIL
2 Tbsp. HONEY
¼ tsp. SALT to taste
2–3 MINT LEAVES (optional)
WATERMELON CUBE, MINT LEAF, and FETA CHEESE CRUMBLES

1. Soak cut onions in water for 15–30 minutes.
2. Combine everything all ingredients in a blender and blend until still slightly chunky.
3. Garnish with a watermelon cube, a mint leaf, and a few feta cheese crumbles.

SAFFRON SEAFOOD SOUP MAKES 8–10 SERVINGS

The crocus sativus is the beautiful flower that shares its stamen so that we can have saffron. This labor-intensive spice only needs a pinch to feel its potency. Watch for cheap imitations such as safflower or Mexican saffron; you'll get the color, but not the flavor.

1 pinch SAFFRON
2 Tbsp. OLIVE OIL
1 ONION, minced
4 CELERY STALKS, chopped
2 cloves minced GARLIC
2–3 quarts FISH STOCK/BROTH
1 sprig FRESH THYME (1/4 tsp. dried)
1 sprig TARRAGON (1/2 tsp. dried)
2 lb. MUSSELS, cleaned
juice from 1 LEMON
SALT

1. In a small dish, add saffron to ¼ cup of cool water and let soak for at least 10 minutes.
2. In a 6-quart or larger stockpot, add olive oil and preheat over medium-high heat until oil starts to shimmer and spread.
3. Add onion, celery, and garlic. Cook until translucent.
4. Add fish stock, thyme, tarragon, and saffron solution. Bring to a slow boil. Let cook for 15 minutes.
5. Add mussels and lemon juice. Mix soup and reduce heat. Cook until mussels start to open, and then immediately remove from heat. Salt to taste.
6. Garnish with crusty sourdough bread and serve immediately.

AMERICAN ONION SOUP MAKES 4 SERVINGS

This update to French onion soup adds some traditional flavors of the American continent: apples, maple syrup, and smoke. For an added treat, serve with pieces of crusty bread.

2 Tbsp. OLIVE OIL
2 sliced ONIONS
2 cloves minced GARLIC
1 finely diced and peeled GRANNY SMITH APPLE
½ tsp. DRY RUBBED SAGE
¼ tsp. LIQUID SMOKE
3 cups BEEF STOCK (or 3 cups water and 3 beef bouillon cubes)
2 Tbsp. MAPLE SYRUP
1 tsp. LEMON JUICE
SALT to taste
shredded CHEDDAR CHEESE

1. Combine olive oil, onions, and garlic in a large stockpot (at least 5 quarts) over medium heat. Stir occasionally until onions start to brown (40–50 minutes).
2. Add all other ingredients except cheese. Simmer for 10–15 minutes.
3. Ladle soup into serving vessel. Top with cheese.

CREAMY ROOT VEGGIE SOUP MAKES 8–10 SERVINGS

Root vegetables tend to be at their freshest in early autumn. Use smaller turnips because their flavor is sweeter.

2 lb. YAMS
2 lb. TURNIPS
3 Tbsp. OLIVE OIL
2 SHALLOTS, chopped
3 cloves GARLIC, coarsely sliced
4 cups LOW SODIUM CHICKEN STOCK
2 LEEKS, cleaned and cut into circles, some for the bisque, some to garnish.
5 BAY LEAVES
1 sprig TARRAGON, plus some additional for garnish
1 Tbsp. MAPLE SYRUP
SALT to taste
¼ lb. PANCETTA
¼ cup YOGURT

1. Preheat oven to 400°F.
2. Peel and slice yams and turnips.
3. Toss yams and turnips in 2 tablespoons of olive oil. Place on baking sheet and place in oven until browning starts.
4. In a large stockpot add 1 tablespoon olive oil, shallots, and garlic over medium-high heat. Cook until onions turn translucent.
5. Add yams, turnips, and chicken stock. Bring to a high simmer.
6. Add ¼ cup of cut leeks, bay leaves, and 1 sprig of tarragon.
7. Simmer for 30–45 minutes until middle of largest root vegetable is tender.
8. Remove from heat and add mixture to a food processor in increments. It will probably take 3–4 rounds to puree all ingredients.
9. Add puree back to stockpot.
10. Add maple syrup and salt.
11. In a frying pan, add pancetta and cook until crispy. Remove from heat and place pancetta on a paper towel to dry.
12. Add remaining leeks to frying pan, turn to medium-low heat and cook for 5 to 10 minutes, until leeks are tender.

13. Crumble pancetta.
14. Finely chop any remaining tarragon.
15. Just prior to serving, add yogurt to bisque and stir well.
16. To serve, add bisque to bowl, top with leek rings, pancetta crumbles, and finely chopped tarragon.

NOTE

» Any starchy vegetable will work well with this recipe, be it potatoes, carrots, squash, sweet potatoes, beets, or parsnips. However, if you use parsnips, be sure to trim out the core of larger roots because they tend to be overly bitter.

» Nutmeg, ginger, and cinnamon, in small quantities, can turn dish into a pumpkin pie–flavored soup.

» In order to be a traditional bisque, it is ideal to use fish, lobster, or clam stock. However, it is not readily available in low sodium varieties. Feel free to substitute ocean-based stock if desired.

CREAM OF ARTICHOKE SOUP MAKES 4–6 SERVINGS

Using frozen artichokes instead of canned allows the floral quality of the vegetable to shine through. It works incredibly well as a warm-up in the cold winter months.

1 diced ONION
4 oz. sliced MUSHROOMS
1 Tbsp. EXTRA-VIRGIN OLIVE OIL
8 oz. FROZEN ARTICHOKE HEARTS (not canned)
1 cup CHICKEN STOCK
½ tsp. SMOKED PAPRIKA
1 Tbsp. HONEY
1 tsp. LEMON JUICE
2 heaping Tbsp. SOUR CREAM
SALT

1. In a shallow frying pan, add onion, mushrooms, and olive oil. Cook over medium heat until onion is translucent.
2. In a 4-quart or larger saucepan, add artichokes, chicken stock, paprika, honey, and lemon juice. Bring to a boil and cook until artichokes are tender. Add onion and mushrooms.
3. Puree using either a blender, immersion blender, or food processor.
4. Immediately prior to serving, whisk in sour cream and add salt to taste.

Main Dishes

BLUEBERRY PULLED PORK SANDWICHES MAKES 10–12 SANDWICHES

Barbecue need not be limited to just tomato-based sauce. This version, using blueberries, is a fun way to break away from the traditional and introduce some great color to your sandwich.

- 1/2 tsp. GROUND MUSTARD
- 1/2 tsp. GROUND CUMIN
- 1 tsp. SMOKED PAPRIKA
- 1 Tbsp. SALT
- 3 lb. BONELESS PORK SHOULDER, excess fat trimmed
- 20 oz. FROZEN BLUEBERRIES
- 2/3 cup APPLE CIDER VINEGAR
- 2/3 cup BROWN SUGAR

1. Combine mustard, cumin, paprika, and salt. Mix well.
2. Sprinkle and rub pork shoulder with spice mixture.
3. In a large frying pan, sear all sides of pork shoulder until brown and place in a slow cooker.
4. Add blueberries, vinegar, and brown sugar to a blender or food processor. Process until completely pureed.
5. Add blueberry puree to pork shoulder. Turn slow cooker on to highest setting and let it cook for at least 3 hours.
6. Remove pork from slow cooker and slice into ½-inch thick slices. Add meat back to slow cooker and cook for at least 1 more hour.
7. After cooking, shred using two forks. Serve on sesame seed buns with pickles, tomatoes, and lettuce.

NOTE » You can also use a bone in shoulder, as long as it's 4 or more pounds. Cook as directed above until it's time to slice pork. Slice around bone, taking care not to shave bone fragments off the shoulder. Cook for another hour and pull any excess meat off bone.

GREEK PORK ROAST MAKES 4 SERVINGS

Try to find a pork roast with a little fat marbling inside the meat, and not just on the outside. You'll be rewarded with a much juicier roast.

2 Tbsp. EXTRA-VIRGIN OLIVE OIL
zest from 1 LEMON
juice from 1 LEMON
1 Tbsp. FRESH OREGANO, minced (or 1 tsp. dried oregano)
8 oz. SLICED MUSHROOMS
8 medium PURPLE POTATOES, quartered
1–2 lb. BONELESS PORK LOIN ROAST
1 tsp. salt per pound of PORK LOIN

1. Preheat oven to 250°F.
2. In a small bowl, combine olive oil, lemon zest, lemon juice, and oregano.
3. In a 5-quart or larger oven-safe cooking vessel with a tight fitting lid, combine mushrooms and potatoes. Place pork loin on top of vegetables with fatty side facing up.
4. Pour olive oil/lemon mixture over pork. Spread salt evenly on pork. Put lid on vessel, and place in oven.
5. Cook for 3–4 hours, until pork is tender. Remove lid from vessel 30 minutes prior to serving and increase heat in oven to 350°F. Bake until top of pork starts to brown.
6. Remove from oven and let stand 5–10 minutes prior to serving.

AUTHENTIC CHICKEN CACCIATORE MAKES 4 SERVINGS

Commonly referred to as "hunter chicken," chicken cacciatore is traditionally made with peppers, tomatoes, and mushrooms. Everything after that is just a bonus!

2 Tbsp. EXTRA-VIRGIN OLIVE OIL
2 lb. CHICKEN THIGHS (or 1½ lb. of boneless skinless chicken thighs)
¼ cup FLOUR
8 oz. MUSHROOMS, quartered
1 ONION, diced
3 cloves GARLIC, minced
2 (8-oz.) cans TOMATO SAUCE
1 large BELL PEPPER, chopped and seeds removed
1 Tbsp. FRESH OREGANO (or 1 tsp. dried)
enough CHICKEN STOCK or WINE to cover chicken during braising
SALT
hearty bread to serve with CHICKEN
coarsely chopped BASIL to garnish (optional)

1. Preheat oven to 350°F.
2. Place an oven-safe cooking vessel such as a cast iron French oven on stove on medium-high heat. Add oil. Remove skin from chicken thighs and dredge in flour. Then add chicken to pan. Cook each side until brown, turning once (about 4 minutes per side). Set chicken aside.
3. Add mushrooms to same pan chicken was cooked in. Cook over medium-high heat until mushrooms start to brown and reduce in size (about 10 minutes). Add onion and garlic. Cook until translucent. Add tomato sauce, chopped bell pepper, and oregano to onion/mushroom/garlic mixture and cook for 5–10 minutes.
4. Add chicken back to sauce and add enough stock to just cover the chicken.
5. Cover the vessel and cook in oven until chicken is tender, about 1 hour. Salt to taste prior to serving.
6. Serve with crusty bread and garnish with chopped basil.

FRUTTI DI MARE (ITALIAN SEAFOOD SOUP) MAKES 4 SERVINGS

When buying fresh/uncooked clams and mussels, make sure the shells are completely closed or close within 30 seconds of tapping lightly on the shell. Discard any shellfish that don't close.

- ½ **YELLOW ONION**, finely diced
- 4 cloves **GARLIC**, minced
- 2 Tbsp. **EXTRA-VIRGIN OLIVE OIL**
- 16 oz. **PLAIN TOMATO SAUCE** (no additional herbs/flavors)
- 4 **ROMA TOMATOES**, skins removed and diced (or a 12-oz. can of plain diced tomatoes)
- 2 cups **LIQUID** (either white wine, or seafood stock plus juice from 1 lemon)
- 1 lb. **DRY FETTUCCINE**
- 1 lb. **ASSORTED PEELED SEAFOOD** (shrimp, scallops, and calamari circles all work)
- 1 lb. **BIVALVE SHELLFISH** (mussels or clams)
- **SALT** to taste
- ¼ cup chopped flat leaf/Italian **PARSLEY**

1. Place at least 16 cups (1 gallon) of water in a large stockpot and preheat to a boil.
2. While water is preheating, sauté onion and garlic in olive oil in a large frying pan or sauté pan until translucent and garlic *just* begins to brown.
3. Add tomato sauce, roma tomatoes, and liquid. Simmer for 5–10 minutes.
4. Add fettuccine to boiling water and cook until al dente. Drain.
5. Add seafood and shellfish to tomato mixture. Cook until seafood is done all the way through and bivalves have all opened. Discard any unopened shells. Salt accordingly.
6. Separate fettuccine into 4 bowls and top with seafood mixture.
7. Garnish with parsley.

KEFTEDES (GREEK MEATBALLS IN TOMATO SAUCE) MAKES 4 SERVINGS

This version of a classic Greek dish will have your family shouting, "Opa!"

The Meatballs

1 cup BREAD CRUMBS
½ cup MILK/WATER
1 Tbsp. DRIED MINT (or 2 Tbsp. fresh minced mint)
2 Tbsp. DRIED OREGANO (or 4 Tbsp. fresh minced oregano)
1 tsp. SALT
1 EGG
1 small YELLOW ONION, minced
1 lb. GROUND BEEF or LAMB

The Sauce

2 (14-oz.) cans DICED TOMATOES
4 cloves GARLIC
2 BAY LEAVES
¼ tsp. CINNAMON
¼ tsp. NUTMEG
juice from 1 LEMON
1 cup BEEF/CHICKEN STOCK

1. In a large bowl, combine bread with ½ cup liquid (milk or water). Add mint, oregano, salt, egg, and onion. Mix well. Add ground meat and mix until everything is combined.
2. Form meat into golf ball–size balls, and cook in a large nonstick frying pan until at least two sides are brown.
3. While meatballs are browning, start sauce by combining tomatoes, garlic, bay leaves, cinnamon, nutmeg, lemon, and stock in a large slow cooker at its highest setting. Mix well.
4. Place browned meatballs in tomato sauce and cook until meatballs are done all the way through (at least 1 hour).
5. Serve with pita bread or rice.

KOREAN DRUMSTICKS MAKES 4 SERVINGS

Boiling the drumsticks prior to putting them in the oven creates a tender, fall-off-the-bone chicken.

8 DRUMSTICKS (2–3 lb.)
1 (1-inch) piece FRESH GINGER, peeled
5 cloves GARLIC, peeled
1 small YELLOW ONION, peeled and quartered
1/3 cup SOY SAUCE
2 Tbsp. SESAME SEED OIL
1/3 cup BROWN SUGAR
1 Tbsp. SRIRACHA SAUCE (optional)
SESAME SEEDS
GREEN ONION, sliced

1. Bring a gallon of water to boil, add drumsticks to water, and cook for 30 minutes. Remove from water, and let cool for 10 to 15 minutes.
2. Combine ginger, garlic, onion, soy sauce, sesame oil, sugar, and sriracha in a blender. Add drumsticks to a large gallon-size bag (may need 2 bags depending on the size of drumsticks). Add marinade from blender to bag. Seal bag, place in a dish, and put in a fridge for at least 1 hour, turning bag over periodically to distribute marinade.
3. After chicken has marinated, preheat oven to 400°F. Place chicken on a nonstick cookie sheet. Coat chicken pieces with any leftover marinade. Bake until chicken reaches an internal temperature of 165°F (40–50 minutes).
4. Sprinkle with sesame seeds and green onion slices to garnish.

NOTE » If desired, this chicken can be cooked on a gas grill. Just turn the grill to its lowest setting and cook until the drumsticks reach an internal temp of 165°F.

CHICKEN YAKITORI SALAD MAKES 4 SERVINGS

Yakitori means "grilled" or "skewered" in Japanese. This version, converted into a salad, has all the flavor of traditional yakitori, but in a healthier form.

1 cup RICE WINE VINEGAR
½ cup SOY SAUCE
¼ cup BROWN SUGAR
8 whole CHICKEN TENDERLOINS
3 CUCUMBERS, either run lengthwise through a mandoline or cut into circles
2 CARROTS, either run lengthwise through a mandoline or cut into circles
1 Tbsp. TOASTED SESAME SEEDS

1. Preheat a gas grill on low.
2. Combine rice wine vinegar, soy sauce, and brown sugar. Mix well. Separate evenly into two bowls.
3. Cook tenderloins over low heat. Cook halfway through and then turn. Lightly brush tenderloins with ½ of rice wine vinegar mixture multiple times, until chicken is completely cooked and mixture is gone.
4. Combine carrots, cucumbers, and sesame seeds. Top with remaining ½ rice wine vinegar mixture.
5. Separate vegetables into 4 portions, and top each salad with 2 cooked chicken tenderloins.

SUMMER SQUASH LASAGNA MAKES 6–8 SERVINGS

I rarely grow summer squash in my garden because I know I'll get zucchini after zucchini during the peak of its season. This is a great way to use all that extra squash.

4–5 whole SUMMER SQUASHES, cut lengthwise in 1/4-inch strips (zucchini or crookneck work well), enough to make 3 layers of zucchini in a 9 x 13 pan
1/4 cup SALT
2 cups SPAGHETTI SAUCE
1 cup RICOTTA CHEESE
1 cup MOZZARELLA SHREDS

1. In a large stockpot, add at least 16 cups (1 gallon) of water. Add salt to it. Bring water to a boil.
2. Add squash and cook until just tender (4–5 minutes). Remove from heat and drain well.
3. Preheat oven to 350°F.
4. In a 9 x 13 pan, place a layer of squash. Gently spread 1/3 of ricotta cheese and 1/3 of spaghetti sauce over it. Repeat until at least 3 layers are in place. Top generously with mozzarella cheese.
5. Place in oven for 30–45 minutes, until cheese is melted and brown. Remove from oven and let rest for at least 10 minutes before cutting and serving.

NOTE » Instead of boiling, omit salt and lightly spray each piece of summer squash with cooking spray and then cook on a grill set to low heat. Cook for 2–3 minutes per side. Layer like noodles as listed above.

RED, WHITE, AND BLUE BURGER MAKES 4 BURGERS

A patriotic way to eat your burger!

1 whole RED PEPPER
1 lb. GROUND BEEF, preferably 90/10 beef.
1/4 cup BLUE CHEESE CRUMBLES
SALT AND PEPPER
4 HAMBURGER BUNS
RED LEAF LETTUCE

1. Preheat your grill.
2. While grill is preheating, place whole red pepper on the grill, turning when pepper skin turns black.
3. Combine beef and blue cheese crumbles and mix well. Divide into 4 equal parts.
4. Press beef into patties and place on grill. Add salt and pepper.
5. While burgers are cooking, remove charred skin from red pepper. Remove seeds and stem from pepper and cut into fillets.
6. Once burgers are fully cooked, remove and place on top of bun. Add red leaf lettuce and red pepper fillets and enjoy!

FALL-OFF-THE-BONE RIBS MAKES 4–6 SERVINGS

Starting these ribs in your slow cooker for a few hours and then finishing them on the grill makes them more tender than those found in the best of restaurants.

5–6 lb. either SHORT or BABY BACK PORK RIBS, cut into 3–4 rib segments
1 Tbsp SALT per pound of ribs
enough WATER to cover the ribs in a slow cooker
½ ONION, sliced

1. In a slow cooker layer the rib segments, salting each layer as you go.
2. Cover with water and add onion. Cook on highest setting for 2–3 hours.
3. Remove from slow cooker and transfer to a grill, cooking over high heat for at least 5 minutes per side.
4. Move to low heat and slather with Pineapple Zing Barbecue Sauce (see below). Let rest over low heat for 5–10 minutes.

PINEAPPLE ZING BARBECUE SAUCE MAKES 2 CUPS

This sauce is *guaranteed* to put some zing in your step!

1 (20-oz.) can PINEAPPLE TIDBITS, IN SYRUP
⅓ cup BROWN SUGAR
¾ tsp. SALT
1 tsp. COARSE PREPARED MUSTARD
½ tsp. CHIPOTLE PEPPER
¾ tsp. coarse GROUND BLACK PEPPER

1. Place all ingredients in a blender or food processor. Process until completely pureed.
2. Place puree in a 2- to 4-quart saucepan over low heat and reduce until thickened (reduce by approximately ⅓). Should yield roughly 2 cups of sauce.

SLOW COOKER LAMB SHANKS MAKES 2–3 SERVINGS

Lamb shanks can be found at specialty butcher stores or some grocery stores with on-site butcher staff.

2 Tbsp. OLIVE OIL
2–3 LAMB SHANKS (as many as will comfortably fit in your slow cooker)
½ tsp. GROUND CUMIN
2 cloves GARLIC
3 sprigs ROSEMARY
1 (12-oz.) can DICED TOMATOES
1 cup pitted BING CHERRIES
1 Tbsp. FLOUR
4 cups CHICKEN STOCK or WATER, plus extra to cover the meat in the slow cooker
1 cup DRIED APRICOTS
1 lb. RED POTATOES
2 Tbsp. KOSHER SALT

1. Preheat a large frying pan over medium-high heat. Add olive oil. Sear lamb shanks on all sides until brown and place in a slow cooker. Add cumin, garlic, rosemary, and tomatoes.
2. Combine cherries, flour, and chicken stock in a blender and puree.
3. Add cherry sauce to slow cooker with enough extra water to cover meat.
4. Add dried apricots, potatoes, and salt.
5. Cook on high for 2–3 hours, until lamb is fall-off-the-bone tender.

TILAPIA WITH LIME RAITA MAKES 4–6 SERVINGS

Tilapia is a fast-growing freshwater fish with a white flaky texture. Yogurt enhances the natural flavor of the fish.

1 cup YOGURT
¼ cup chopped FRESH CILANTRO
1 Tbsp. FRESH LIME JUICE
1 tsp. SALT
1 Tbsp. OLIVE OIL
4–6 TILAPIA FILLETS
SALT AND PEPPER

1. Prior to cooking, combine yogurt, cilantro, lime juice, and salt. Cover and place in a fridge while tilapia cooks.
2. Preheat olive oil in a large nonstick frying pan over medium heat. Add tilapia with light salt and pepper. Cook through (3–5 minutes per side). (Depending on your pan size you may need to cook in shifts.)
3. Place tilapia fillets on a bed of salad greens and drizzle yogurt mixture over it.

BACON WRAPPED STEAK DOGS MAKES 4 DOGS

A man-pleasing version of the traditional hot dog. A great dish to serve around Father's Day.

2 SIRLOIN STEAKS
4 strips THIN CUT BACON
1/4 cup APRICOT PRESERVES/JAM
1 Tbsp. SRIRACHA SAUCE
4 HOAGIE-STYLE BUNS
diced CILANTRO

1. Cut each steak lengthwise into two equal pieces. Wrap each steak piece with one piece of bacon. Secure the bacon ends with toothpicks.
2. Grill or pan fry steak dogs until bacon is crispy, turning once (about 5 minutes per side). Remove toothpicks.
3. While steak is cooking, combine apricot and sriracha. Mix well.
4. Place cooked steak inside either a hoagie or hotdog bun and top with apricot hot sauce and cilantro.

TANDOORI CHICKEN TENDERS MAKES 4–6 SERVINGS

The overnight marinade in yogurt and spices tenderizes the chicken and enhances its juiciness.

2 tsp. GARAM MASALA (either store-bought, or made as per the recipe on the next page)
1 tsp. CAYENNE (medium spiciness) or 1 tsp. CHILI POWDER (low spiciness)
2 cups PLAIN YOGURT
4 tsp. SEA SALT
1 tsp. PAPRIKA
2 Tbsp. FRESH GRATED GINGER
2 lb. CHICKEN TENDERLOINS
1 RED ONION, cut into rings
2 RED PEPPERS, cut into rings
OLIVE OIL
minced CILANTRO

1. At least 6 hours before serving, place Garam Masala in a nonstick frying pan. Cook over medium heat, stirring occasionally until it smells fragrant (4–5 minutes).
2. In a nonreactive storage vessel (plastic, glass, or stainless steel), add Garam Masala, cayenne/chili powder, yogurt, salt, paprika, and grated ginger. Mix until thoroughly combined.
3. Make 3 shallow cuts in each piece of chicken, and then add to yogurt/spice mixture. Mix well, making sure the chicken is completely covered with yogurt. Cover and refrigerate for at least 5 hours, but no more than 24 hours.
4. Combine peppers and onions. Drizzle with olive oil. Mix well to make sure vegetables are evenly coated. Preheat grill to high heat for at least 15 minutes (if you have a grill thermometer, at least 500°F). Generously grease grill, place tenderloins on the grill, and cook until completely done, turning once (8–12 minutes). While the chicken is cooking, place onions and peppers on grill and cook until heated thoroughly.
5. Serve family style on a large platter. Place chicken first and then peppers and onions. Garnish with cilantro. Serve with fresh tortillas, naan, or basmati rice.

GARAM MASALA MAKES 1 TABLESPOON

Literally translated as "hot mix," this spice mixture combines spices with a little bit of kick, and a whole lot of flavor. The fresher your spices, the more pungent your Garam Masala.

1 tsp. GROUND CINNAMON
½ tsp. GROUND BLACK PEPPER
½ tsp. CUMIN
½ tsp. GROUND FENNEL SEED
½ tsp. GROUND CARDAMOM

1. Combine all spices and use as directed in Tandoori Chicken Tenders recipe (see opposite).

STEAK OSCAR MAKES 2 STEAKS

Each steak you cook has a secret, a hidden mystery if you will, about when it's done. Careful observation of how it cooks will tell you how pink/red/brown the inside is.

- 2 STEAKS of your choosing (rib eye, tenderloin, New York, or sirloin all work well)
- 6 oz. CRAB MEAT (about 3/4 cup)
- 1/4 cup TOASTED PINE NUTS
- 2 LIMES
- 1 AVOCADO
- 4 slices PROVOLONE CHEESE

1. Generously salt and pepper both sides of your steak prior to placing in a pan.
2. Cook steak just shy of desired temperature on one side, and then flip.
3. While steak is cooking, put crab meat directly onto pan. Top with pine nuts and juice of two limes. After crab meat has warmed through, separate it into two portions. Top each steak with 3 ounces crab meat per steak and ½ of an avocado, cut into slices. Top each steak with 2 slices of provolone cheese and cover. May need to add an ice cube to pan with steak to steam cheese until it's cooked completely through.
4. If desired, garnish with lime zest.

NEW ORLEANS–STYLE MEATLOAF MAKES 6–8 SERVINGS

Spice up your meatloaf with the flavors of the French Quarter. If you can't find Andouille, substitute with either kielbasa or chorizo.

2 Tbsp. OLIVE OIL
8 oz. ANDOUILLE SAUSAGE, ground (about 1 cup)
1 cup CHOPPED ONION
1 RED BELL PEPPER, finely chopped
1 HOT RED PEPPER (cayenne or chipotle)
2 GARLIC CLOVES, finely minced
1/2 tsp. DRIED THYME
1/2 tsp. DRIED OREGANO
1/2 cup TOMATO SAUCE
1/2 cup BEEF BROTH
1/4 cup FRESH BREAD CRUMBS
2 EGGS
2 lb. GROUND BEEF
1 tsp. SALT, to taste
1 tsp. BLACK PEPPER, to taste

1. Heat olive oil in a large skillet over low heat. Add sausage, onion, bell pepper, hot pepper, garlic, thyme, and oregano. Mix well. Cover and cook for 15 minutes.
2. Place in a bowl and let cool to room temperature. Add tomato sauce, broth, and bread crumbs to sausage mixture.
3. Whip eggs, and then add to sausage mixture. Crumble ground beef into bowl. Add salt and pepper. Mix gently until combined.
4. Pack into a 5 x 9 loaf pan. Bake at 350°F for 45 minutes, or until cooked through (internal temperature of 165°F). Pour off drippings from pan. Cover pan loosely with foil and let stand for 10 minutes. Slice and serve.

HAWAIIAN FISH TACOS MAKES 6–8 SERVINGS

Pacific salmon is much richer in both color and flavor than Atlantic salmon, and freezes incredibly well. If you can't find it in the butcher's section of the store, look in the frozen food aisle.

- 3/4 cup sliced MUSHROOMS
- 1/2 MEDIUM YELLOW ONION, sliced
- 3/4 cup segmented FRESH PINEAPPLE (or an 8-oz. can, drained)
- 1 Tbsp. SOY SAUCE
- 1/2 PEELED MANGO
- 4–6 LARGE STRAWBERRIES
- 1 lb. PACIFIC SALMON, cut into 1-inch strips
- 1/4 cup CHOPPED CILANTRO
- 1/2 cup COCONUT MILK
- 6–8 8-inch FLOUR TORTILLAS
- 2 LIMES, cut into wedges

1. Preheat an 8-inch or larger frying pan over medium heat. Add mushrooms and cook until they start to give off moisture. Add onions and pineapple. Stir occasionally. As onions start to turn translucent, add soy sauce and cook until all liquid is gone from bottom of pan and onions start to brown.
2. Slice mango and strawberries and add to a separate bowl. Set aside.
3. In another frying pan, 9 inches or larger, add salmon. Generously salt salmon. Turn each individual strip once it looks like it's cooked about halfway through.
4. While salmon is cooking, combine chopped cilantro with coconut milk. Mix well.
5. To serve, layer onion mixture, salmon strips, and mango salsa down the center of a tortilla. Top with coconut/cilantro dressing and a squeeze of lime from a lime wedge.

Hawaiian Fish Taco Salad:

» Prepare all ingredients as described above except for tortillas. Preheat oven to 325°F. In an inverted cupcake pan, push tortillas in between cupcake cups, making sure bottoms of tortillas are flat. Bake until tortillas start to brown. Serve as above, but include shredded lettuce.

BRIE AND FIG GRILLED CHEESE SANDWICH MAKES 2 SANDWICHES

Grilled cheese sandwiches are a staple of the American lifestyle. This old standby, usually made with Wonder bread and processed American cheese, could benefit from a little TLC. The recipe calls for brushed olive oil, but you can substitute butter. Just keep in mind that butter is 10–20 percent water, and your toasted bread won't be quite as crisp as bread toasted with olive oil.

¼ cup FIG PASTE/JAM
¼ tsp. CHIPOTLE POWDER (optional)
4 thinly sliced pieces of SOURDOUGH BREAD
2 Tbsp. EXTRA-VIRGIN OLIVE OIL
enough thinly sliced BRIE CHEESE to cover two slices of bread
¼ cup ARUGULA

1. Combine fig preserves with chipotle powder. Mix well.
2. Lightly brush one side of each slice of sourdough bread with olive oil, and set two slices of bread on a pan or griddle preheated to 350–400°F (medium heat). Add layers of brie on top of each bread slice.
3. Add arugula directly on top of cheese.
4. Spread fig/chipotle jam on unoiled sides of remaining slices of bread, and place fig/chipotle jam bread slices on top of arugula, jam side down.
5. Cook sandwich for approximately 5 minutes per side, or until both sides are brown and cheese is melted.

TROUT FILLETS WITH A GINGER APPLE SLAW MAKES 4 FILLETS

If trout is out of season or too expensive, feel free to substitute with salmon.

1 RED PEPPER
1 tsp. LEMON JUICE
2 cups WATER
2 GRANNY SMITH APPLES
2 Tbsp. BALSAMIC VINEGAR
2 Tbsp. EXTRA-VIRGIN OLIVE OIL
4 TROUT FILLETS (salmon and halibut also work well)
2 inches FRESH GINGER (peeled and finely chopped)
2 handfuls ARUGULA
SALT AND PEPPER

1. Roast red pepper in either an oven, on a grill, or over a gas stove (see notes below). Set in fridge to cool. Once pepper has cooled, remove as much skin as possible. Remove seeds and chop pepper into small pieces.
2. Combine lemon juice and water in a large bowl. Slice apples into thin slices and add to lemon water. Let soak for 10 or more minutes. Whisk together vinegar and oil.
3. Preheat oven to 350°F. Bake trout fillets on a greased cookie sheet until a fork or knife inserted into the middle of the fish flakes the fish apart (15–20 minutes).
4. Drain apples out of lemon water. Discard lemon water. Combine apple, ginger, red pepper, and ½ of vinegar/olive oil.
5. Toss arugula in remaining vinegar/oil. Serve by putting down a bed of arugula, placing fish on top of arugula, and topping with ginger apple slaw. Salt and pepper to taste.

How to roast a red pepper:

» Oven: Slice peppers in half and remove seeds. Place on cookie sheet. Broil until skin is blistered and black.

» Barbecue: Place directly over heat and turn as pepper blisters. Please note, the skin on a pepper cooked on the grill may not get black and blistery. Don't cook more than 15 minutes.

» Gas stove: Place red pepper directly over flame and turn using tongs as pepper skin turns black.

FIGGY PORK CHOPS MAKES 4 SERVINGS

Fresh figs cooked in brown butter with sage—one of the most decadent ways to serve pork chops.

4 center cut PORK CHOPS
4 Tbsp. BUTTER
5 fresh SAGE LEAVES, minced
8 quartered FRESH MISSION FIGS
juice 1/2 LEMON

1. Pan fry pork chops until they reach an internal temperature of at least 160°F.
2. Remove pork chops, put them on a plate, and cover plate loosely with foil.
3. Add butter and sage to now empty pork chop pan and cook over medium heat until butter starts to turn brown. Turn heat to low and add figs and lemon juice. Stir just until figs are warm.
4. Remove pork chops from foil. Top with quartered figs and a generous amount of brown butter sauce.

NEW DELHI MEATBALLS MAKES 4 SERVINGS

Jazz up your meatballs with all the flavor of India. If you're cooking for little ones, omit the chili flakes.

- 3/4 cup plain PANKO BREAD CRUMBS
- 1/2 cup MILK
- 1 lb. GROUND BEEF (or LAMB)
- 2 Tbsp. minced FRESH GINGER
- 1 EGG
- 1/2 cup COCONUT
- 1 tsp. CINNAMON
- 1/2 tsp. NUTMEG
- 1/2 tsp. GROUND CARDAMOM
- 1 tsp. GROUND PEPPER
- 1 Tbsp. SALT
- 1/4 cup PEANUT BUTTER (optional)
- 1 Tbsp. CHILI FLAKES (optional)

1. Combine bread crumbs and milk. Mix and set aside for 5 minutes.
2. In a separate bowl, combine all remaining ingredients: ground meat, ginger, egg, coconut, cinnamon, nutmeg, cardamom, pepper, salt, peanut butter, and chili flakes.
3. Add milk and bread crumbs to meat mixture. Mix all ingredients thoroughly.
4. Preheat large frying pan on medium or medium-low heat. Form meat into teaspoon-size meatballs and cook until done (about 7 minutes per side).
5. Serve over rice with Cilantro Yogurt (see recipe below).

CILANTRO YOGURT MAKES 1 CUP

Commonly referred to as "raita," this cooling sauce helps your mouth handle the heat of spicy food.

- 1 cup UNFLAVORED YOGURT
- 1/4 cup finely minced CILANTRO LEAVES

1. Combine yogurt and cilantro. Mix well. Serve with New Delhi Meatballs.

COLA BRAISED COUNTRY RIBS MAKES 12 SERVINGS

Country ribs aren't actually ribs, but parts of the shoulder cut to look like rib meat. They tend to be fairly tough and flavorful. When cooked in cola, the liquid tenderizes the meat, and enhances the natural flavor of the pork.

6 lb. PORK SPARE RIBS, trimmed of excess fat
2 cloves GARLIC, minced
1 YELLOW ONION, minced
6 CARROTS, cut into 1-inch chunks
6 CELERY STALKS, cut into 1-inch chunks
1 (12-oz.) can COLA (not diet)
1 Tbsp. minced FRESH ROSEMARY
4–6 BAY LEAVES
enough CHICKEN STOCK to cover the meat
SALT

1. Working in a large stockpot or enameled Dutch oven, sear outside of ribs until brown. You may need to do this in multiple batches.
2. Once ribs are brown, remove and set aside. Add garlic, onions, carrots, and celery to stockpot and cook until onions are translucent.
3. Add ribs back into pot, as well as cola, rosemary, bay leaves, and enough chicken stock to just cover meat.
4. Bake at 325°F in oven for 2½ to 3 hours. Salt to taste and serve with Cola Gravy (recipe below).

VARIATION

» Try other sodas like Lemon Lime, Root Beer, or Dr. Pepper. They're all are delicious!

COLA GRAVY MAKES 1 CUP

Topping your ribs with cola gravy adds both richness and sweetness to your ribs.

1 cup LIQUID FROM COLA BRAISED COUNTRY RIBS, run through a strainer
1 Tbsp. CORNSTARCH
½ tsp. SALT

1. Combine liquid and cornstarch while cold. Put in a sauce pan over high heat, whisking frequently until boiling. After mixture boils, reduce heat to low and add salt.

BACON CHEESEBURGER PIZZA MAKES 6–8 SERVINGS

Although dill pickles aren't traditionally considered a pizza topping, they'll make all the difference in this fun and flavorful pizza.

The Pizza Dough (Makes 2 crusts)

½ tsp. SUGAR
1 pkg. RAPID RISE YEAST
1 cup WARM WATER (100–110 degrees)
1 Tbsp. OLIVE OIL
2 Tbsp. WHITE VINEGAR
2½ tsp. SALT
2½ cups FLOUR (+/- ¼ cup based on humidity)
extra FLOUR for rolling out the crust

The Toppings

1 sliced ONION
SALT to taste
8 oz. EXTRA LEAN GROUND BEEF (about 1 cup)
SPAGHETTI SAUCE of your choice
½ cup grated MONTEREY JACK CHEESE
1 cup grated CHEDDAR CHEESE
6 slices of BACON, precooked and diced
40 PICKLE SLICES (optional)

1. In a large bowl, dissolve sugar and yeast in water. Wait 10 minutes until all yeast is dissolved/proofed.
2. Add oil, vinegar, salt, and flour and stir in a mixer until incorporated. Mix on a medium speed for approximately 5 minutes until dough forms a cohesive ball.
3. Cover with a damp cloth and store in a warm, humid place for 1½ to 2 hours.
4. Divide dough into 2 equal portions. Roll each portion into a ball. You want a dough ball without visible seams on top. Cover dough balls with damp cloth and let rise for at least 1 hour.
5. Over extremely low heat, put sliced onions in a saucepan and cover. Stir occasionally until onions start to brown (about 45 minutes). Add salt and remove from heat.

6. While onions are cooking, add beef to a separate frying pan and cook until browned. Add salt as needed.
7. Preheat oven to 500°F (or higher).
8. Place a dough ball on a lightly floured surface and dust some flour on top. Using rolling pin, roll out a thin circle, using lots of flour on both sides to prevent sticking.
9. Top with spaghetti sauce and grated cheeses. Add ½ of ground beef, ½ of bacon, and ½ of onions. Add 20 or so pickle slices to the pizza. Repeat steps 8 and 9 for second pizza.
10. Place a pizza on a baking sheet on bottom rack of oven for 10–15 minutes, or until bottom of crust is golden. To check doneness, gently lift pizza using either a fork or a spatula to reveal underside of crust. The pizza is done when the underside has considerable browning.

CHICKEN AND CHERRIES MAKES 4 SERVINGS

This is a great way to use cherries when they're in season, though frozen cherries are a great substitute. The sweetness of the cherries contrasts incredibly well to the savory flavor from the chicken bouillon cube.

4 SPLIT CHICKEN BREASTS
1 lb. CHERRIES, pitted (fresh or frozen both work)
4 BASIL LEAVES (or 1 tsp. dried basil)
½ cup ORANGE JUICE
1 CHICKEN BOUILLON CUBE
2 Tbsp. DICED ONION
1 Tbsp. EXTRA-VIRGIN OLIVE OIL

1. Cook chicken breasts using your method of choice (grill, fry, and so on) until done.
2. While the chicken is cooking, combine cherries, basil, orange juice, and bouillon cube in a blender or food processor.
3. Add onions to a frying pan with olive oil and cook until translucent.
4. Add onions to cherry mixture and puree.
5. After plating chicken, spoon cherry sauce over it.
6. Garnish with basil and fresh cherries.

VARIATIONS

» Add 1 teaspoon chipotle powder for a spicy/smoky flavor.

» After pureeing cherry mixture, add ½ ounce of unsweetened chocolate and heat over low heat, stirring until the chocolate is completely melted.

ZINGER DOGS MAKES 8 SERVINGS

Hot dogs have become "haute dogs" with this zesty slaw. Once you try ginger and apple on top of your hot dog, you'll never go back to ketchup and mustard.

8 ALL-BEEF HOT DOGS
2 Tbsp. grated FRESH GINGER
1 GRANNY SMITH APPLE, grated
1 Tbsp. HONEY
juice from 1 LEMON
8 BUNS
ARUGULA

1. Heat grill and cook hot dogs.
2. While hot dogs are cooking, combine ginger, apple, honey, and lemon juice.
3. When hot dogs are done, divide apple/ginger slaw evenly among hot dogs, and top with arugula.

SPICY HAWAIIAN DOGS MAKES 8 DOGS

The tangy quality of pineapple pairs well with the Italian sausage on these hot dogs. If serving to kids, use mild Italian sausage.

8 ITALIAN SAUSAGES
8 BUNS
1 MANGO
½ cup MINCED PINEAPPLE
1 AVOCADO, cubed
juice from 1 LIME
1 Tbsp. OLIVE OIL
SALT to taste
1 tsp. minced CILANTRO (reserve some whole leaves as a garnish)

1. Grill sausages until completely cooked. Once they're done, place each sausages in a bun.
2. While completing previous step, combine mango, pineapple, avocado, lime juice, olive oil, and salt.
3. Spoon mango salsa evenly among cooked sausage. Garnish with a couple of cilantro leaves.

ORANGE CHICKEN BURGUNDY MAKES 4–6 SERVINGS

This traditional French recipe is made kid friendly by adding orange juice in the place of red wine.

1 Tbsp. EXTRA-VIRGIN OLIVE OIL
4 slices good quality BACON, chopped
½ cup FLOUR
2 lb. CHICKEN BREASTS, cut into 1½- to 2-inch pieces
½ YELLOW ONION, minced
2 cloves GARLIC, minced
8 oz. MUSHROOMS, quartered
3 ribs CELERY, chopped
2 Tbsp. chopped FRESH THYME (4 to 5 sprigs)
1 Tbsp. FRESH ROSEMARY (about a 6-inch length of a sprig)
1 Tbsp. FRESH OREGANO (about 3 little bunches)
2 cups ORANGE JUICE
3 Tbsp. CORNSTARCH
1 cup CHICKEN STOCK
2 cups FROZEN PEARL ONIONS
SALT AND PEPPER
CHIVES for garnishing

1. Heat a large stockpot or enameled cast iron pot over medium heat. Add olive oil and bacon and cook until bacon is crisp. Remove with a slotted spoon. Set on a paper towel to drain.
2. While bacon is cooking, put flour on a large plate. Dredge chicken pieces in flour. Toss chicken to coat and remove any excess flour.
3. Add chicken to hot bacon drippings. Cook until brown (3 to 4 minutes per side).
4. Add yellow onions, garlic, mushrooms, celery, thyme, rosemary, and oregano. Let cook until onions are translucent (5 to 10 minutes).
5. Add orange juice. Combine cornstarch and chicken stock before adding to the pot. Whisk well to eliminate any chunks.
6. Add cornstarch/chicken stock to the pot and mix well. Add pearl onions.
7. Cook until sauce is thickened and onions are cooked through. Salt and pepper to taste. Serve over noodles, and garnish with bacon and chives.

COCONUT CHICKEN CURRY MAKES 6–8 SERVINGS

Coconut is a common ingredient in South Indian curries. This version was taught to me in Hyderabad India in a 10 x 10 foot house, using the floor as our cutting board, stove, and table. Though it's been updated to reflect ingredients found in North America, it's soul remains Indian.

1 Tbsp. OIL
½ YELLOW ONION, diced
1 clove GARLIC, minced
2 tsp. chopped FRESH GINGER
2 cups WATER
1 lb. BONELESS SKINLESS CHICKEN BREASTS, cut into cubes
1 JALAPEÑO PEPPER, finely minced (optional)
½ cup UNSWEETENED COCONUT (desiccated is preferred over flaked)
¼ cup CREAMY PEANUT BUTTER
¼ tsp. CINNAMON
¼ tsp. NUTMEG
¼ tsp. CARDAMOM
¼ tsp. CUMIN
¼ tsp. BLACK PEPPER
½ tsp. CAYENNE PEPPER (adjust to your tongue's ability to handle heat)
¼ tsp. TURMERIC
½ cup YOGURT
1 Tbsp. LIME JUICE
SALT
finely chopped CILANTRO

1. In an 6-quart or larger stockpot, combine oil and onions over medium-low heat. Cook until onions start to turn translucent. Add garlic and ginger and cook until fragrant.
2. Add water, chicken, and jalapeño. Cover. Simmer until chicken is cooked through.
3. In a frying pan over medium heat, add coconut and cook until golden brown, stirring frequently throughout cooking time. Remove from heat. Add peanut butter, cinnamon, nutmeg, cardamom, cumin, black pepper, cayenne pepper, turmeric, yogurt, and lime juice.
4. Once chicken is completely cooked, add peanut/coconut mixture to chicken and stir well. Add salt to taste before serving, and garnish with finely chopped cilantro.

INSIDE-OUT CHICKEN PARMESAN MAKES 4 SERVINGS

When slicing your chicken breast to create the pocket, use a knife sharp enough to make one continuous slice. You'll have more control and end up with a better pocket to stuff the chicken breast.

½ cup minced SUN-DRIED TOMATOES
2 cloves GARLIC, minced
½ cup shredded MOZZARELLA
½ cup shredded PARMESAN
¼ cup BREAD CRUMBS
2 Tbsp. CAPERS
1 Tbsp. CAPER JUICE (the liquid that surrounds the bottled capers)
1 (4-inch) sprig of FRESH ROSEMARY, minced (or 2 tsp. dried and minced rosemary)
½ Tsp. SALT
4 CHICKEN BREASTS, each weighing approximately 8 oz.

1. Preheat oven to 400°F.
2. Combine tomatoes, garlic, mozzarella, parmesan, bread crumbs, capers, caper juice, rosemary, and salt. Mix well. Separate stuffing into 4 equal portions.
3. Carefully slice each breast in half horizontally, taking care not to slice all the way through. The goal is to create a stuffing pocket.
4. Take 1 portion of stuffing and pack it tightly into a ball. Insert ball into middle of 1 chicken breast, sealing with toothpicks as necessary. Repeat with other chicken breasts.
5. Bake in oven until cheese stuffing reaches 165°F (about 30 minutes).

EGGPLANT PARMESAN BURGERS MAKES 4 SERVINGS

Ground chuck is the best beef to make burgers with. Taste study after taste study reveals that chuck is the flavor most people associate with a hearty burger. Adding fresh rosemary and oregano just enhances its natural flavor!

1 lb. 85% lean/15% fat GROUND CHUCK
½ cup BREAD CRUMBS
1 EGG
1 Tbsp. FRESH ROSEMARY, finely chopped
1 Tbsp. FRESH OREGANO, finely chopped
1 medium EGGPLANT
SALT (for eggplant and grilling patties)
2 CIABATTA LOAVES
GARLIC POWDER
1 small bag SUN-DRIED TOMATOES
1 (5-oz.) container FRESHLY GRATED PARMESAN CHEESE BLEND

1. Combine chuck, bread crumbs, egg, rosemary, and oregano. Stir. Divide ground chuck mixture into 4 portions and make into patties.
2. Peel eggplant. Cut into enough ¼-inch thick slices to cover 4 burgers. Sprinkle eggplant slices with salt, and then cook in a single layer in microwave until tender (about 3 minutes).
3. Cut ciabatta loaves into "burger-size" buns. Then cut a horizontal slice on each bun and brush olive oil on interior.
4. Cook patties on grill, liberally applying salt and garlic powder, turning when juice starts to form on top of each burger. Put eggplant slices on grill. 3 minutes after putting eggplant on grill, put enough grilled eggplant on burgers to cover each patty.
5. Gently place sun-dried tomatoes on top of eggplant. Liberally sprinkle with cheese. Add buns, oiled side down on grill and cook until toasted.
6. Cover the grill. Continue to cook until patties are cooked all the way through and cheese is melted.
7. Pull buns off grill, add patty, and for an added punch, try adding fresh whole basil leaves.

QUICK AND CRISPY ROAST CHICKEN MAKES 4 SERVINGS

The key to crispy chicken skin is high heat. But in most recipes, too high heat causes the chicken skin to burn before the inside is cooked. But by removing the backbone of the chicken with kitchen shears and flattening it out, the inside cooks quickly, resulting in a juicy bird with crispy skin.

1 (2½–4 lb.) **FRYER CHICKEN**
1 Tbsp. **SEA/KOSHER SALT**
2 Tbsp. **OLIVE OIL**
1 **ONION**, quartered
2 cups **CHICKEN STOCK**

1. Preheat oven to 500°F.
2. Turn chicken so breast side is down. Using kitchen shears or sharp scissors, cut along either side of chicken spine, and remove it from chicken. Place chicken skin-side down on a cutting board, with thighs spread open. Push down on thighs and legs until middle bone (keel bone) snaps. Chicken should now lie flat.
3. Sprinkle salt on top of chicken and let it sit for 10–15 minutes.
4. Add olive oil to an oven-safe frying pan and preheat oil over high heat. Place chicken skin-side down in frying pan, taking care to spread chicken out evenly across pan. Place another pan on top of chicken and cook for 5 minutes.
5. Remove pan from top of chicken. Flip chicken so skin side is up.
6. Add onions and chicken stock to pan.
7. Put pan in oven and cook until chicken reaches an internal temperature of 165°F. (35–40 minutes).
8. Let chicken rest for 5 minutes before cutting and serving.

PIZZA BIANCO MAKES 4 PIZZAS

"White pizza," named for the lack of tomato sauce, is a fun way to break the traditional pizza mold. When you're making the garlic oil, keep the heat relatively low to prevent the garlic slices from browning.

The Pizza Dough (Makes 4 crusts)

½ tsp. SUGAR
½ tsp. YEAST
1 cup WARM WATER (100–110 degrees)
1 Tbsp. OLIVE OIL
2 Tbsp. WHITE VINEGAR
½ cup AMERICAN LAGER (think Budweiser or O'Doul's)
2½ tsp. SALT
4½ cups FLOUR
extra FLOUR for rolling out the crust

The Toppings

2 cups BALSAMIC VINEGAR
4 Tbsp. EXTRA-VIRGIN OLIVE OIL
8 cloves GARLIC, minced
4 Tbsp. minced FRESH ROSEMARY
2 lb. MOZZARELLA CHEESE

1. In a large bowl, dissolve sugar and yeast in water. Wait 10 minutes until all yeast is dissolved.
2. Add oil, vinegar, lager, salt, and flour. Stir in a mixer until incorporated. Mix on a medium speed for approximately 5 minutes until dough forms a cohesive ball. Cover with a damp cloth and store in a warm humid place for 1½ to 2 hours.
3. Divide dough into 4 equal portions. Roll each portion into a ball. You want a dough ball without visible seams on top.
4. In a 1-quart or larger saucepan, add balsamic vinegar and cook over low heat until vinegar has reduced to approximately ½ cup.
5. Preheat oven to 500°F or higher. Put oven rack on lowest shelf.
6. Over medium-low heat, combine olive oil, garlic, and rosemary in a frying pan. Cook for 2–3 minutes, or until garlic is translucent.

7. Place a dough ball on lightly floured surface and dust some flour on top. Using rolling pin, roll out a thin circle, using lots of flour on both sides to prevent sticking.
8. Spread oil/garlic/rosemary mixture over top of crust. Grate cheese and top pizza with ¼ of cheese. After topping pizza, carefully slide it into oven.
9. Bake in oven for 10–15 minutes, until bottom of crust is golden. To check doneness, gently lift pizza using either a fork or a spatula to reveal underside of crust. Pizza is done when underside has considerable browning.
10. Drizzle 2 tablespoons of balsamic reduction over pizza. Repeat steps with remaining dough balls.

MUSTARD AND MOLASSES PORK LOIN (M&M) MAKES 6–8 SERVINGS

Molasses-braised pork is smoky and sweet. The mustard gives it just a hint of danger, without being too spicy.

3–4 lb. PORK LOIN ROAST
2 Tbsp. SALT
2 Tbsp. COOKING OIL
1 ONION, sliced
8 oz. MUSHROOMS (about 1 cup)
½ cup WATER
8 medium RED POTATOES
½ cup WATER
1 Tbsp. MOLASSES
1 Tbsp. COARSE DIJON MUSTARD

1. Preheat oven to 250°F. Remove roast from fridge and sprinkle liberally with salt 30 minutes before cooking.
2. In a large (6-quart or larger) cast iron Dutch oven with a tight fitting lid, preheat cooking oil over high heat. Add pork roast and brown all sides.
3. Turn roast so side with fat cap is facing upwards. Add onions, mushrooms, and potatoes. Then add water.
4. Combine molasses and mustard in a small bowl. Spread mixture over top of roast.
5. Cover Dutch oven. Bake in oven for approximately 2 hours, until center of roast reaches 160°F.
6. Remove lid from Dutch oven and turn oven to broil. Broil meat and vegetables until meat is brown and bubbly (about 5 minutes).

PECAN CRUSTED CHICKEN STRIPS MAKES 4 SERVINGS

Southern style chicken strips made easy! The brown sugar and chipotle combination gives your strips a sweet, smoky flavor. If you're serving kids, replace the chipotle powder with smoked paprika.

- ½ cup FLOUR
- 3 EGGS
- 1 Tbsp. SOY SAUCE
- 2 Tbsp. MILK
- 1 cup PANKO BREAD CRUMBS
- 1 cup FINELY GROUND/CHOPPED PECANS
- 2 Tbsp. BROWN SUGAR
- 1 tsp. GROUND CHIPOTLE PEPPER (optional if you're serving kids that don't like a kick to their food)
- 2 tsp. SALT
- 2 lb. CHICKEN BREASTS, cut lengthwise into ½-inch wide strips

1. Set up 3 separate breading tubs, one containing flour; another containing eggs, soy sauce, and milk; and another containing panko, pecans, brown sugar, pepper, and salt.
2. Divide chicken strips into 4 equal batches. Flour each batch, immerse in egg, and then transfer to pecan/panko breading, taking care to let egg drip off prior to putting in panko breading. Continue process until all chicken is coated.
3. Place on a well-oiled baking sheet and bake for 18–20 minutes, turning halfway through.
4. Upon removal from oven, immediately transfer to a cooling rack to retain crispness.
5. Discard any remaining flour, egg, or breading.

NOTE

» If you have nut allergies, replace pecans with an equivalent amount of panko crumbs.

CRAB STUFFED PORK CHOPS MAKES 4 SERVINGS

The pork chop can get a little boring. But by adding crab, this recipe takes advantage of two naturally occurring ingredients in each meat that works together, making each meat taste better than before. Inosinate and Glutamic acid combine to create richness.

1 (6-oz.) can LUMP CRAB MEAT, drained
¼ cup BREAD CRUMBS
1 EGG
1 Tbsp. ANCHOVY PASTE
½ tsp. SESAME OIL
½ tsp. SALT
1 stalk CELERY FINELY, minced
1 half MEDIUM ONION, diced
5 MUSHROOMS, minced
4 PORK LOIN PORK CHOPS, butterflied

1. Preheat oven to 350°F.
2. Combine lump crab, bread crumbs, egg, anchovy paste, sesame oil, and salt in a medium bowl. Set aside.
3. Combine celery, onion, and mushrooms in a frying pan and sauté until mushrooms lose all moisture. Add celery mixture to crab mixture and stir to combine.
4. Divide stuffing into 4 equal parts and add to 1 side of a butterflied pork chop. Fold other side of pork chop over, put on a lightly greased baking sheet, and cook until stuffing reaches 160°F (30–45 minutes).

EASY CHICKEN SALTIMBOCCA MAKES 4 SERVINGS

My mother-in-law, Patti, calls this "my chicken." This is one of those dishes that will knock your taste buds out of the back of your head, only to have them scurrying back to your tongue to get another taste. It's a well balanced blend of sweet, sour, salt, and savory. Be sure to give the prosciutto time to get crispy.

4 split BONELESS SKINLESS CHICKEN BREASTS, trimmed of fat
2 Tbsp. OLIVE OIL
12 large SAGE LEAVES, 8 of them minced
½ cup FLOUR
1 Tbsp. FRESHLY GROUND BLACK PEPPER
6 oz. THINLY SLICED PROSCIUTTO (8 total slices)
1 finely MINCED SHALLOT
1 cup WHITE WINE (Chardonnay preferred) or replace with 1¼ cup ORANGE JUICE (omit lemon juice if using orange juice).
juice from 1 LEMON (roughly 1 tsp.)
4 Tbsp. BUTTER, cut into small chunks
SALT

1. Lay chicken breasts on a cutting board and slice each one horizontally, turning them into two large cutlets.
2. Preheat oven to 200°F.
3. Add olive oil to a large frying pan over medium-high heat. Place 4 whole sage leaves in olive oil and let fry for 25–30 seconds. Remove leaves from pan.
4. Combine flour and black pepper. Dredge chicken cutlets in flour, sprinkle minced sage over top, and cover with a slice of prosciutto.
5. Place chicken, prosciutto-side down, into frying pan, turning when chicken is cooked halfway through. Depending on the size of your pan, you may need to repeat this 3–4 times until all cutlets are cooked. When chicken is cooked through, place in an oven-safe dish and keep warm in oven.
6. Add minced shallot to frying pan, stirring until shallot becomes translucent and starts to brown.
7. Add wine and lemon juice to frying pan, stirring to remove all brown bits from bottom of pan.
8. Finish beurre blanc (butter sauce) by adding butter 1 chunk at a time, whisking vigorously with each addition and not adding another until previous chunk is completely melted.
9. Salt sauce to taste. Serve chicken over rice or noodles, topping with beurre blanc and fried sage leaf.

NEW YORK–STYLE MARGHERITA PIZZA MAKES 6 SERVINGS

My wife and I were in Little Italy for the Feast of San Gennaro and had the perfect Margherita pizza. I've made pizza after pizza, trying to recreate that amazing balance of crispy crust, melting cheese, and fresh basil. Here it is!

The Pizza Dough

- ½ tsp. SUGAR
- ½ tsp. YEAST
- 1 cup WARM WATER (100–110 degrees)
- 1 Tbsp. OLIVE OIL
- 2 Tbsp. WHITE VINEGAR
- ½ cup AMERICAN LAGER
- 2½ tsp. SALT
- 4½ cups FLOUR
- extra FLOUR for rolling out the crust

The Toppings

- 1 (28-oz.) can DICED TOMATOES WITH BASIL ADDED (San Marzano DOP preferred).
- 2 lb. thinly sliced FRESH MOZZARELLA, preferably from buffalo's milk
- 5 sprigs FRESH BASIL, sliced into shreds

1. In a large bowl, dissolve sugar and yeast in water. Wait 10 minutes until all yeast is dissolved.
2. Add oil, vinegar, lager, salt, and flour and stir in a mixer until incorporated. Mix on a medium speed for approximately 5 minutes until dough forms a cohesive ball.
3. Cover with a damp cloth and store in a warm, humid place for 1½ to 2 hours.
4. Divide dough into 4 equal portions. Roll each portion into a ball. You want a dough ball without visible seams on top.
5. Put pizza stone on middle rack in 500°F or higher oven to preheat. (The hotter oven can get, the better.)
6. Place a dough ball on lightly floured surface and dust some flour on top. Using a rolling pin, roll out a thin circle, using lots of flour on both sides to prevent sticking. Place rolled-out dough on pizza stone (careful, stone will be hot).
7. Top with diced tomato and thinly sliced mozzarella. After topping pizza, carefully slide it into the oven.

8. Bake in oven for 10–15 minutes, until bottom of crust is golden. To check doneness, gently lift pizza using either a fork or a spatula to reveal underside of crust. Pizza is done when underside has considerable browning.
9. Top with a generous amount of sliced fresh basil.

NOTE

» Simmer tomatoes for over low heat for 30 minutes to 1 hour to remove as much liquid as possible.

» A word of caution on working with a pizza stone. It should be *hot* in order to appropriately sear bottom of pizza. When done working with it, let pizza stone cool to touch before attempting to wash. If washed too soon, cold water will shock stone, causing it to crack. Further, don't use anything other than water to clean stone. Soap would work its way in and make future pizzas taste like Palmolive.

» If you choose to omit beer, increase water to 1½ cups.

Desserts

CARAMEL APPLE UPSIDE-DOWN CAKE MAKES 6–8 SERVINGS

The “cake” portion of this is a cross between a pound cake and a spiced cookie, a perfect base to top with apples and caramel.

The Apples

2 GALA APPLES, peeled, cored, and sliced
1 Tbsp. FRESH GINGER, minced
1 Tbsp. LEMON JUICE
2 Tbsp. BUTTER

The Cake

3/4 cup BROWN SUGAR
6 Tbsp. MELTED BUTTER
2 LARGE EGGS
1 cup FLOUR
1 dash SALT

The Caramel

3/4 cup SUGAR
1/4 cup CORN SYRUP
1 Tbsp. LEMON JUICE
1 tsp. CINNAMON

1. Combine apples, ginger, and lemon juice in a large bowl. Add enough water to cover. Let sit while making cake and caramel.
2. Start cake in a mixing bowl by creaming together brown sugar and butter. Add eggs, flour, and salt. Mix until combined. Set aside.
3. Drain water from apples and ginger. In a large frying pan, add 2 tablespoons butter to pan and heat until butter starts to brown. Add apples and cook, taking care not to break apple slices.
4. In a saucepan, start caramel by combining sugar, corn syrup, lemon juice, and cinnamon. Heat on low until sugar is dissolved and liquid starts to brown.
5. While sugar/lemon is cooking, butter a 9 x 2 round cake pan. Add a layer of parchment paper cut to fit bottom of pan. Butter top layer as well. Arrange apples in bottom of cake pan. Add sugar/lemon mixture. Top with cake batter.
6. Cook in a 350°F oven for 15–20 minutes or until a toothpick inserted into cake comes out clean. Remove from oven. Run a knife around exterior of cake to separate it from pan. Let cake cool for 30 minutes on a baker's rack.
7. Place a plate large enough to cover cake dish over cake pan. Invert cake pan and serve cake off of plate.

EASY BAKLAVA MAKES 24–36 CUPS

My Lebanese grandma spent *hours* making fresh fillo dough that was only ready when it was so thin you could place it over a love note and still read the words of adoration. Fortunately, this recipe simplifies the long arduous process of making baklava while still maintaining the integrity of the dish.

The Fillo Cup

8 oz. PREMADE FILLO DOUGH
1/2 cup UNSALTED BUTTER, melted

The Filling

1 cup WALNUTS
1 cup BLANCHED ALMONDS
1/2 cup SUGAR
2 Tbsp. MELTED BUTTER
1/2 tsp. CINNAMON
1/4 tsp. NUTMEG
1/4 tsp. LEMON ZEST

The Syrup

1 cup SUGAR
3/4 cup WATER
1 tsp. LEMON JUICE
2 drops ORANGE OIL (or 1 tsp. ORANGE EXTRACT)

1. Carefully brush 10 sheets of fillo dough with butter, creating a 10-layer-sheet thick pastry. Place a damp towel on fillo sheets not being used to prevent them from drying.
2. Cut 10-layer pastry into 3-inch squares (12 squares per sheet), using either kitchen shears or a pizza cutter. Repeat process, creating 1 additional 10-layer pastry cut into squares (you may have a few extra fillo sheets).
3. Put fillo pastry squares into a mini cupcake pan, pressing each square to bottom of each cup.
4. Combine walnuts, almonds, sugar, butter, cinnamon, nutmeg, and lemon zest in a food processor, and pulse until nuts are coarsely ground.

5. Spoon nut mixture directly into fillo cups. Bake at 350°F until fillo cups are browned (30–40 minutes).
6. While cups are baking, combine sugar, water, and lemon juice. Bring to a boil. Simmer for 10 minutes, and then add orange oil/extract. Let cool.
7. Spoon syrup directly onto nut portion of dessert and let stand for 1 hour before serving.

GRILLED PEACH HAND PIES MAKES 3–4 PIES

Peach hand pies are a southern tradition. They're normally fried in butter to get the crisp shell. However, cooking them on the grill infuses a gourmet feel without all the calories of deep frying.

The Butter Pie Crust

1¼ cups FLOUR
½ tsp. SALT
1½ tsp. SUGAR
1 stick COLD BUTTER, chopped into 8 pieces
2 Tbsp. WATER

The Filling

2 PEACHES, peeled, pit removed, and each peach cut into 8 pieces
COOKING SPRAY
2 Tbsp. BROWN SUGAR
1 tsp. VANILLA
¼ tsp. CINNAMON
pinch of SALT
extra WHITE SUGAR for sprinkling

1. Sift together flour, salt, and sugar. Combine dry ingredients with cold butter in a food processor and pulse until combined. (Alternately, use a handheld pastry blender to combine [it helps to freeze butter], and then grate it prior to mixing.)
2. Add water and mix by hand until just combined. Form into a disc and wrap in plastic wrap. Place in fridge for at least 30 minutes.
3. Preheat grill until it reaches 400°F (medium heat on a gas grill usually works best).
4. Lightly coat peaches with cooking spray and place on grill, cooking for approximately 5 minutes. Then remove and place in a bowl.
5. Remove pastry dough from fridge and roll disc out into a circle approximately ⅛ inch to ¼ inch thick. Cut 5-inch circles out of crust (I use the lid from a #10 coffee can). Pastry disc should yield 3–4 pastry shells.
6. Add brown sugar, vanilla, cinnamon, and salt to peaches. Gently mix.

7. Carefully spoon peach filling into a pastry shell, taking care to keep filling at least ¼ inch from edge of pastry shell. Wet 1 side of pastry with a finger, and fold pie shell together. Crimp with a fork and sprinkle with sugar. Repeat for remaining pastry shells.
8. Add pies to grill, cooking each side until brown (7–10 minutes per side). Let cool and serve.

GRILLED STRAWBERRY SHORTCAKE MAKES 4–6 SERVINGS

Grilling store-bought angel food cake gives it a homemade feel without spending hours making your own cake. When combined with grilled strawberries and reduced balsamic vinegar, it becomes out of this world!

1 cup BALSAMIC VINEGAR
2 lb. STRAWBERRIES
1/3 cup WHITE VINEGAR
1 ANGEL FOOD CAKE
EXTRA-VIRGIN OLIVE OIL
1/4 cup SUGAR
ICE CREAM or WHIPPED CREAM

1. Over low heat, reduce balsamic vinegar until it is ¼ of its original volume. Set aside.
2. 30 minutes before grilling, clean and trim strawberries. Place in a large nonreactive vessel at least one gallon in size. Add 16 cups (1 gallon) water and white vinegar. Let soak for 30 minutes.
3. Meanwhile, cut angel food cake into 8–12 equal slices. Drizzle/brush each cut side with olive oil.
4. Drain strawberries in a colander and toss with sugar.
5. On a preheated grill set at medium to low heat, place each piece of cake on grill, and cook until lightly browned (about 2 minutes per side).
6. Place berries on grill. Cook until warmed through and sugar has been dissolved (4–5 minutes).
7. Plate 2 pieces of cake, strawberries, and top with ice cream or whipped cream. Drizzle with balsamic reduction.

EASY MINT CHOCOLATE CAKE MAKES 8–10 SERVINGS

A good chocolate cake should be more chocolate than cake. In this version, the chocolate is the star, with just enough mint to balance out the chocolate's richness.

- **10 oz.** SEMISWEET CHOCOLATE
- **1 cube** BUTTER
- **5** EGGS
- **1¼ cup** SUGAR
- **5 Tbsp.** FLOUR
- **1½ tsp.** BAKING POWDER
- **1 tsp.** MINT EXTRACT

1. Preheat oven to 325°F.
2. In a saucepan over low heat, melt chocolate and butter. Stir frequently.
3. While chocolate/butter are melting, combine eggs and sugar in a separate bowl and mix until creamy and pale yellow. Sift flour and baking powder into egg/sugar mixture and mix to combine.
4. Once chocolate is completely melted, gently fold it into egg/sugar mixture. Stir in mint extract.
5. Pour batter into a buttered and floured 9-inch springform pan.
6. Bake for 20 minutes, and then lightly cover with aluminum foil and bake for 30 minutes more.
7. Garnish with crushed mint candy canes and whipped cream.

THE ULTIMATE BUTTER CARAMEL MAKES 40–50 1-INCH SQUARE CARAMELS

Temperature is everything in this recipe. Cook it too cold and you may end up with caramel sauce, cook it too hot and you'll have jawbreakers. Be careful as you approach your target temperature, as the heat of the caramel rises, so does the speed of its rise. Turn your head and you may be 5°F hotter than your target!

2 cups LIGHT CORN SYRUP
2 cups DARK BROWN SUGAR (light brown sugar doesn't work)
1/2 cup SALTED BUTTER, cut into small chunks
1/8 tsp. SALT
2 cups HEAVY CREAM
1 tablespoon VANILLA

1. Combine corn syrup and dark brown sugar in large saucepan. (I use a 6-quart pan.) Place on medium heat and stir until dissolved. Increase heat to high and bring to a boil. Let mixture boil for 2–3 minutes, keeping sides of pan clean.
2. Add butter 1 chunk at a time, stirring constantly. Add salt. Keep stirring as you slowly pour in cream so mixture does not stop boiling. *Stop stirring* after cream is completely incorporated. Cook without stirring to 236°F (see note below about changes to final temperature based on elevation) and take off of heat. Add vanilla. Without scraping pan, pour into a generously buttered 9 x 12 pan. (I use Pyrex as it makes it easier to remove next day.) Put pan on a cooling rack and let cool for 12 or more hours. Cover pan with plastic wrap after 1–2 hours of cooling.
3. Turn pan over onto a cutting surface and caramel block should slowly fall on to surface. If not, try heating bottom of pan in hot tap water or, if all else fails, gently helping it out with a rubber spatula.
4. Cut caramel into squares and wrap in waxed paper.

VARIATIONS

» Smoked Sea Salt Caramel—Substitute 1/8 teaspoon salt with 1 teaspoon smoked sea salt (apple wood preferred). Add a couple of drops of liquid smoke.

» Chocolate Caramel—Finely chop 3 ounces of unsweetened bakers chocolate. After removing from heat, add vanilla as directed, and then add chocolate and stir until all chocolate is incorporated and you have a consistent-looking caramel.

NOTE

» Your elevation is important in getting this recipe correct. Therefore, cook to following temperature based on your elevation:

SEA LEVEL TO 1000 FEET	244 DEGREES F
1000–2000 FEET	242 DEGREES F
2000–3000 FEET	240 DEGREES F
3000–4000 FEET	238 DEGREES F
4000–5000 FEET	236 DEGREES F
5000–6000 FEET	234 DEGREES F
6000 AND ABOVE	SUBTRACT 1 DEGREE FOR EVERY 500 FEET IN ELEVATION RISE

PEACH "AWESOME" MAKES 6 SERVINGS

Grilled peaches are pretty awesome by themselves, but when you add a goat cheese mousse and a drizzle of reduced balsamic vinegar, it takes awesome to an entirely new level.

½ cup BALSAMIC VINEGAR
¾ cup COLD WHIPPING CREAM
1 (4-oz.) pack FRESH GOAT CHEESE (chèvre)
⅓ cup SUGAR
zest from 1 LEMON (about 4 tsp.)
6 PEACHES, cut in half and pit removed

1. Over low heat, add vinegar to a small saucepan and reduce by ¾.
2. While vinegar is reducing, add whipping cream to a clean bowl and whip to hard peaks.
3. In a food processor, combine goat cheese, sugar, and lemon zest with ¼ of whipped cream. Process until pureed.
4. Fold goat cheese mixture into whipped cream. Set aside in fridge.
5. 15 minutes before serving, place peaches cut side down on a lightly oiled barbecue grill set on low. Cook just until brown grill marks form (8–10 minutes).
6. To serve, put two peaches on a plate, top with a dollop of whipped goat cheese, and drizzle vinegar reduction over it.

NOTE

» If reduction is too thick, put pan back over low heat for a couple of minutes and sauce will thin out enough to drizzle.

TRADITIONAL "CUSTARD" ICE CREAM BASE MAKES 1 QUART

When making ice cream, the faster you can get your ice cream base to freeze, the smoother the ice cream will be. Therefore, chill your ice cream base for an extended period of time prior to putting it in the ice cream maker. And don't be afraid to fill up your ice cream maker less than you normally would. You'll get smoother ice cream!

4 cups HALF AND HALF (or 2 cups SKIM MILK and 2 cups CREAM)
1 cup SUGAR
8 EGG YOLKS
2 Tbsp. CORNSTARCH
2 tsp. VANILLA

1. In a medium saucepan, add 3 cups of half and half and 1 cup of sugar. Heat over medium heat.
2. In a large bowl, combine remaining 1 cup of half and half, egg yolks, cornstarch, and vanilla. Mix well.
3. Cook half and half until it starts to simmer. Slowly add hot half and half mix to egg yolk/half and half mixture. Place the entire mix back in saucepan and cook until mixture starts to thicken. Be careful to keep it from boiling.
4. Once mixture has thickened, pour it through a strainer, cover it, and put it in fridge until chilled. Freeze according to manufacturer's directions with ice cream maker. Remove from ice cream maker and freeze 2 hours before serving.

EASY ICE CREAM BASE MAKES 1 QUART

When you're in a hurry, this version of an ice cream base is a great way to get ice cream without heating up the kitchen.

- 4 cups **HALF AND HALF** (or 2 cups **SKIM MILK** and 2 cups **CREAM**)
- 3/4 cup **SUGAR**
- 1 small pkg. **VANILLA PUDDING**

1. Combine half and half, sugar, and vanilla pudding. Put it in ice cream maker and freeze according to manufacturer's directions. Put ice cream in freezer 2 hours before serving.

VARIATION

» Make into brown sugar ice cream by replacing white sugar in recipe with brown sugar.

S'MORE ICE CREAM MAKES 1 QUART

All the flavors of a campfire s'more, without the smelly clothes.

- **ICE CREAM BASE**, prepared to add to ice cream maker
- 1/8 tsp. **LIQUID SMOKE**
- 1/2 cup **MINI CHOCOLATE CHIPS**
- 1 cup **MARSHMALLOWS**
- 1/2 cup **CHOPPED GRAHAM CRACKERS**

1. As the ice cream base starts to harden in the ice cream maker, stop the mixer and add liquid smoke, chocolate chips, marshmallows, and graham crackers. Continue freezing according to directions. Remove ice cream from mixer. Place in a freezer for 2 hours before serving.

CONCORD GRAPE SORBET MAKES ¾ QUART

Concord grapes have a musky flavor that makes them difficult to use for anything other than juice. Adding some lime and sugar enhances the natural sweetness, while still maintaining the unique identity of the grape.

2 qt. CONCORD GRAPES, stemmed
½ cup SUGAR
juice from 2 LIMES

1. After washing and stemming all grapes, separate into 2 or 3 batches and add each batch to blender. Blend at a high speed until broken down and pour mixture through strainer to remove all grape solids.
2. Repeat for all batches. Add sugar and lime to grape juice, mixing well until sugar is dissolved.
3. Place in refrigerator for at least 2 hours. Add mixture to a 2-quart ice cream maker and mix according to manufacturer's instructions.
4. Once set, remove from ice cream maker and transfer to a freezer-safe vessel. Cover and freeze for at least 2 more hours.

NOTE

» Although this recipe is designed for a 2-quart ice cream maker, it only makes about a ¾ quart of sorbet (a larger cooling surface is required to quickly freeze the juice and reduce the formation of ice crystals, resulting in a silky smooth mouth feel). If you have a larger ice cream maker, feel free to increase the recipe accordingly, remembering that your final product should be no more than ½ the capacity of the ice cream maker.

CUCUMBER AND CANTALOUPE SORBET MAKES 4–6 SERVINGS

When cucumber season hits, it hits with a vengeance! When choosing cucumbers, look for consistent shape and color, since irregular-shaped cucumbers tend to be a bit more bitter.

3 CUCUMBERS, peeled, seeded, and cut into ½-inch slices
½ CANTALOUPE, peeled, seeded, and cut into cubes.
juice from 1 LEMON
½ cup SUGAR

1. Divide cucumbers and cantaloupe into small batches, and then puree in a blender. Strain puree through a fine mesh sieve and discard solids. Add lemon juice and sugar. Stir until dissolved.
2. Place mixture in a 2-quart ice cream maker and prepare according to the directions of ice cream maker.
3. Once solid, transfer to freezer for at least 1 hour to completely harden.

ORANGE MERINGUE COOKIES MAKES 24–36 MERINGUES

Orange oil is usually found in your baker's aisle at the grocer. In the event you can't find it, most specialty stores carry it next to their candy-making supplies.

2 EGG WHITES
½ tsp. VANILLA
⅛ tsp. CREAM OF TARTAR
⅔ cup SUGAR
2 drops of ORANGE OIL (or ¼ tsp. ORANGE EXTRACT)

4. Make sure mixing bowl is absolutely clean.
5. Preheat oven to 300°F.
6. Beat egg whites, vanilla, and cream of tartar until mixture forms soft peaks. Add sugar in small batches, beating until stiff peaks form. Add orange oil (or extract) and mix using a rubber spatula.
7. Place on a parchment-covered baking sheet using a rounded teaspoon 2 inches apart.
8. Bake for approximately 20 minutes, until firm and bottom is lightly browned. Transfer parchment paper to a cookie rack and let cool.

CHOCOLATEY SOUFFLÉ MAKES 4 SOUFFLÉS

Soufflés have a bad name. Maybe it's the terrible reputation they have for falling at the drop of a feather, or the scolding your mother gave you if you spoke louder than a whisper when they were in the oven. Here's the thing: There is *nothing* to be afraid of. Neither walking past the oven nor yelling will cause a soufflé to fall.

- 2 Tbsp. BUTTER
- 2 Tbsp. SUGAR
- 4 oz. SEMISWEET CHOCOLATE (about 1/2 cup)
- 1 Tbsp. BUTTER
- 2 EGG YOLKS
- 3 EGG WHITES
- 1/4 tsp. CREAM OF TARTAR
- 1/3 cup POWDERED SUGAR

1. Preheat oven to 400°F.
2. Use 2 tablespoons of butter to line four 7-ounce ramekins and use and 2 tablespoons of sugar coat insides. Place in refrigerator.
3. Melt chocolate and butter over low heat, stirring until completely melted. Remove from heat and whisk in egg yolks. Return chocolate mixture to stove and heat over low heat, taking care not burn chocolate.
4. In a clean bowl, combine egg whites and cream of tartar. Whip until soft peaks form. Add powdered sugar to egg whites and continue to whip until hard peaks form.
5. Divide egg whites into 4 portions and gently fold the egg whites into melted chocolate, taking care not to stir the mixture (only fold).
6. Fill each ramekin 2/3 full with mixture, and put in oven. Set timer for 8 minutes.
7. Once 8 minutes have elapsed, reduce oven temperature to 350°F and cook for another 5–6 minutes. Remove from the oven, let cool for 5 to 10 minutes, and eat ASAP.

VARIATION » For a fun variation, insert a small square of dark chocolate into center of soufflé right as it comes out of oven.Your soufflé will turn into a delicious molten chocolate soufflé.

CHEWY CHOCOLATE CHIP COOKIES MAKES 3–4 DOZEN COOKIES

Melting the butter, making the batter, and then chilling significantly reduces the amount of air captured in your dough. Less air means dense and chewy cookies.

2 sticks BUTTER (make sure your sticks are the $\frac{1}{4}$ lb. variety for a total of $\frac{1}{2}$ lb. butter)
$2\frac{1}{2}$ cups FLOUR
1 tsp. SALT
1 tsp. BAKING SODA
$\frac{1}{4}$ cup SUGAR
$1\frac{1}{4}$ cups BROWN SUGAR
1 EGG
1 EGG YOLK
2 Tbsp. MILK
$1\frac{1}{2}$ tsp. VANILLA EXTRACT
1 (12-oz.) bag MILK CHOCOLATE CHIPS

1. Heat oven to 350°F.
2. Melt butter in a medium saucepan over low heat. Sift together flour, salt, and baking soda. Set them aside.
3. Pour melted butter in mixer's work bowl. Add sugar and brown sugar. Cream butter and sugars on medium speed. Add egg, yolk, milk, and vanilla extract. Mix until well combined. Slowly incorporate flour mixture until thoroughly combined. Stir in chocolate chips.
4. Chill dough, and then scoop onto parchment-lined baking sheets, 6 cookies per sheet (each one about the size of a golf ball). Bake for 11 minutes or until golden brown, checking cookies after 5 minutes. Rotate baking sheet for even browning. Cool completely and store in an airtight container.
5. For an added zing, top each cookie with a few crystals of either fleur de sel, or coarse sea salt.

TIPS

» Brown sugar will absorb water when left in a relatively humid environment, which is why it's included in this recipe. It guarantees a chewy texture.

» After dry ingredients are added, beat cookie dough a minimal amount. You barely want to incorporate the flour. Anymore and you'll have a tough cookie.

» Baking on parchment or silpat will make it easier to get cookies off baking sheets as soon as they come out of oven. Leaving cookies on cookie sheets after that will cause bottoms of cookies to be overdone.

» Make sure brown sugar is *really* well packed. Not packing it enough can cause the cookies to fall flat.

» Another common challenge with these cookies is an oven that isn't preheated, or calibrated properly. If first tray of cookies are flat, try increasing oven temperature to 375°F.

BRIE APPLE PIE MAKES 1 PIE

Browning your apples *before* putting them in your pie enhances the richness of the apple and also makes your pie less soupy. Feel free to pile the apples as high as you want because the precooking virtually eliminates any oven shrinking.

juice from 1 LEMON
8–10 MEDIUM APPLES
¼ cup BUTTER
1 cup BROWN SUGAR
1 Tbsp. FLOUR
1 tsp. CINNAMON
pinch SALT
2 PIE CRUSTS
thinly sliced BRIE CHEESE
1 EGG WHITE
1 Tbsp. SUGAR
¼ tsp. CINNAMON

1. Preheat oven to 350°F.
2. Fill a nonreactive bowl approximately 2 inches full with water. Add lemon juice.
3. Peel, core, and slice apples, immersing them in lemon water for a few minutes, and then transferring them to a colander to drain.
4. Divide apples into 3 even piles. Split butter into thirds. Working one pile at a time, heat a large sauté pan or frying pan with a portion of butter until completely melted and barely starting to turn brown. Add apples, taking care to maintain as much contact between metal and the apples. Cook until apples in contact with pan start to brown. Flip apples, and then brown again. Remove after a fair amount of browning has occurred and reserve. Repeat for remaining two piles.
5. Combine apples with brown sugar, flour, cinnamon, and salt.
6. Place pie crust inside a pie tin, flattening dough against side of tin. Layer ½ of browned apples on pie crust, taking care to minimize air pockets.
7. Add a thin layer of brie cheese, and then top with remainder of apples.
8. Cover with remaining pie crust, flute edges together to create a seal, and cut 5–6 small vent holes on top of crust.

9. Cover edges of pie with either aluminum foil or crust edge guard and bake in oven for 25 minutes.
10. Remove foil/edge guard, brush with egg white, and sprinkle sugar and cinnamon on crust. Bake for 25 more minutes, or until pie crust achieves a golden color.

VARIATIONS

» Crumble some blue cheese (with blue cheese, less is certainly more) and make a layer of apples, a layer of cheese, and then top with remainder of apples and crust, and bake as directed.

» Cut 20 store-bought caramels in half and mix through pie filling.

» Using only one pie crust, place apples in middle, and gently fold crust up and around apples, covering approximately 1 inch of apples and pleating edge as you go. Leave a 6-inch circle of uncovered apples in middle. Brush edges with egg white. Bake for 40–45 minutes uncovered or until crust is brown.

PLUM CRISP FOR TWO MAKES 2 SERVINGS

Plums are loaded with water, baking them in a crisp causes that water to evaporate, and you're left with a super concentrated plum filling that is well balanced by the brittle crust.

4 medium PLUMS, chopped into 1/4-inch to 1/2-inch pieces
1 Tbsp. CORNSTARCH
1 Tbsp. HONEY
2 Tbsp. FLOUR
2 Tbsp. OATMEAL
2 Tbsp. BROWN SUGAR
2 Tbsp. MELTED BUTTER
1/4 tsp. CINNAMON

1. Preheat oven to 350°F.
2. Combine plums, cornstarch, and honey. Separate into two baking dishes (ramekins work best).
3. In another bowl, combine flour, oatmeal, brown sugar, butter, and cinnamon. Mix well.
4. Evenly divide oatmeal mixture and sprinkle over plum mix.
5. Bake for 20–25 minutes, until topping is brown and plum mix starts to bubble.

LEMON CHEESECAKE MAKES 1 CHEESECAKE

The key to keeping your cheesecake from cracking is slowly cooling it down from the oven, which is why the recipe calls for leaving it in the oven after cooking.

The Crust

1 cup GRAHAM CRACKER CRUMBS
3 Tbsp. MELTED BUTTER
1 tsp. LEMON ZEST

The Filling

2 lb. CREAM CHEESE (four 8-oz. packs)
1¼ cup SUGAR
zest from 2 LEMONS, finely chopped
1 tsp. VANILLA
3 Tbsp. FLOUR
4 EGGS
2 EGG YOLKS
½ cup SOUR CREAM
1 Tbsp. LEMON JUICE
pinch of SALT

1. Preheat oven to 375°F.
2. Combine graham cracker crumbs, butter, and lemon zest in a bowl. Mix well. Add to bottom of a 9-inch springform pan that is at least 2 inches tall. Lightly press crust into place.
3. Wrap bottom of pan in aluminum foil, taking care to wrap foil at least 1 inch high all around pan. Bake crust on bottom rack in oven for 7 minutes.
4. While crust is baking, combine all filling ingredients and mix well using either beater attachment on a stand mixer or mixing beaters.
5. Once crust is done, add cream cheese filling to springform pan. Place pan in a baking vessel large enough to hold it. Add enough water to bottom of baking container holding springform pan that water covers 1 inch of springform pan but doesn't rise over edge of aluminum foil.
6. Return cheesecake to bottom rack. Water should go about halfway up sides of pan.
7. Bake at 450°F for 10 minutes, and then reduce heat to 250°F and bake until a toothpick inserted into the middle of the cheesecake comes out clean (about 90 minutes). Let cheesecake cool inside oven with door closed for 60 minutes before transferring to fridge. Chill for at least 3 hours before serving.

Cooking Measurement Equivalents

Cups	Tablespoons	Fluid Ounces
⅛ cup	2 Tbsp.	1 fl. oz.
¼ cup	4 Tbsp.	2 fl. oz.
⅓ cup	5 Tbsp. + 1 tsp.	
½ cup	8 Tbsp.	4 fl. oz.
⅔ cup	10 Tbsp. + 2 tsp.	
¾ cup	12 Tbsp.	6 fl. oz.
1 cup	16 Tbsp.	8 fl. oz.

Cups	Fluid Ounces	Pints/Quarts/Gallons
1 cup	8 fl. oz.	½ pint
2 cups	16 fl. oz.	1 pint = ½ quart
3 cups	24 fl. oz.	1½ pints
4 cups	32 fl. oz.	2 pints = 1 quart
8 cups	64 fl. oz.	2 quarts = ½ gallon
16 cups	128 fl. oz.	4 quarts = 1 gallon

Other Helpful Equivalents

1 Tbsp.	3 tsp.
8 oz.	½ lb.
16 oz.	1 lb.

Metric Measurement Equivalents

Approximate Weight Equivalents

Ounces	Pounds	Grams
4 oz.	¼ lb.	113 g
5 oz.		142 g
6 oz.		170 g
8 oz.	½ lb.	227 g
9 oz.		255 g
12 oz.	¾ lb.	340 g
16 oz.	1 lb.	454 g

Approximate Volume Equivalents

Cups	US Fluid Ounces	Milliliters
⅛ cup	1 fl. oz.	30 ml
¼ cup	2 fl. oz.	59 ml
½ cup	4 fl. oz.	118 ml
¾ cup	6 fl. oz.	177 ml
1 cup	8 fl. oz.	237 ml

Other Helpful Equivalents

½ tsp.	2½ ml
1 tsp.	5 ml
1 Tbsp.	15 ml

TOPICAL INDEX

ABOUT THE AUTHOR

What happens when you mix growing up cooking for a big family, traveling the world, and having a *love* of food? You get Chef Tom Woodbury and a tribute to the science of cooking.

Tom has always been interested in understanding the science of food. When he was six years old, he "experimented" with peanut butter and jelly sandwiches, playing with the ingredients until making the *perfect* sandwich. His fourth grade science fair experiment was on the impacts of differing levels of baking powder, and he determined that more isn't always better. Understanding the way that food performs at a chemical, biological, and molecular level has always been a passion for Tom.

His entire objective is to teach you how to make delicious fresh and easy meals, with a hearty dose of fun, technique, and a little science.

0 26575 14467 3